Student Book

American
Headway
STARTER

D1088399

John and Liz Soars

OXFORD
UNIVERSITY PRESS

OXFORD
UNIVERSITY PRESS
198 Madison Avenue
New York, NY 10016 USA

Great Clarendon Street
Oxford OX2 6DP England

Oxford New York

Auckland Cape Town Dar es Salaam Hong Kong Karachi
Kuala Lumpur Madrid Melbourne Mexico City Nairobi
New Delhi Shanghai Taipei Toronto

with offices in

Argentina Austria Brazil Chile Czech Republic France Greece
Guatemala Hungary Italy Japan South Korea Poland Portugal
Singapore Switzerland Thailand Turkey Ukraine Vietnam

OXFORD is a trademark of Oxford University Press.

Library of Congress Cataloging-in-Publication Data

Soars, John
    Student book American headway starter/John and Liz Soars.
    p.cm.
    ISBN-13: 978 0 19 435387 8
    ISBN-10: 0 19 435387 7
    1. English language—Textbooks for foreign speakers. I. Soars,
Liz II. Title.
PE1128 .S5938 2002
428.2'4—dc21   2002002058

American Headway Starter Student Book:
Editorial Manager: Nancy Leonhardt
Managing Editor: Jeff Krum
Editor: Pat O'Neill
Production Editor: Arlette Lurie
Art Director: Lynn Luchetti
Senior Designers: Claudia Carlson, Shelley Himmelstein
Senior Art Buyer: Jodi Waxman
Photo Researcher: Donatella Accardi
Production Manager: Shanta Persaud
Production Coordinator: Eve Wong

Printing (last digit): 10 9 8 7 6

Printed in China.

Acknowledgments

Cover concept: Rowie Christopher
Cover design: Rowie Christopher and Silver Editions

Illustrations and realia by Adrian Barclay, Lisa Berkshire, Mark Blade, Carlos
Castellanos, Matthew Cooper/Debut Art, Ben Croft/The Art Collection,
Paul Daviz/Illustrationweb.com, Graham Humphries/The Art Market,
Marie-Helène Jeeves/Central Illustration Agency, Scott MacNeill/MacNeill
& Macintosh, Di Mainstone/Central Illustration Agency, Kate Miller/Central
Illustration Agency, Karen Minot, Lisa Parett, Gavin Reece/New Division,
Nicola Slater, Sparky, William Waitzman, Mark Watkinson

*The publishers would like to thank the following for their permission to
reproduce photographs:* L. Adamski/GettyOne Stone; AKG London; Alaska
Stock; Nigel Atherton/Stone; Bill Bachman/Index Stock; G. Bass/GettyOne
Telegraph; Gale Beery/Index Stock; V. Besnault/GettyOne Telegraph;
Bettman/Corbis; Biblioteca Reale, Turin, Italy/Leonardo da Vinci Self-
Portrait, c. 1513/The Bridgeman Art Library; James P. Blair/PhotoDisc;
C. Borland/Photolink/PhotoDisc/Picturequest; Peter Bowater/Alamy; M.
Brigdale/Anthony Blake Photo Library; British Library, London/Shakespeare/
The Bridgeman Art Library; K. Brofsky/GettyOne Stone; BSIP Agency/Index
Stock; A. Buckingham/GettyOne Stone; Gay Bumgarner/Index Stock; Burke/
Triolo/Brand X Pictures/PictureQuest; G. Buss/GettyOne Telegraph; G. Butera/
GettyOne Stone; S. Carmona/Corbis; Myrleen Cate/Index Stock; Dwight R.
Cendrowski/MIRA; Chauvet/Jerrican/Science Photo Library; Jason Childs/
FPG; Christine Osborne Pictures; Christopher Moore Ltd.; Clint Clemens/
International Stock; Nick Clements/FPG; Geoffrey Clifford/The Image Bank;
Stewart Cohen/Index Stock; comstock.com; Corbis; corbisstockmarket.com;
Tobi Corney/Stone; P. Craven/Robert Harding Picture Library; Dennis
Curran/Index Stock; J. Darell/GettyOne Stone; D. Day/GettyOne Stone;
P. Dazeley/GettyOne Stone; D. Degnan/Corbis; M. Del Grosso/Alamy.com;
G. & M. David de Lossy/The Image Bank; George B. Diebold/The Stock-
market; M. Douet/GettyOne Stone; C. Ehlers/GettyOne Stone; Chad Ehlers/
ImageState; A. Errington/GettyOne Stone; L. Evans/GettyOne Stone; L. Evans/
OUP; Eyewire Collection; D. Falconer/PhotoLink/PhotoDisc; M. Fearn/Press
Association; Fernandez and Peck/ImageState; K. Fleming/Corbis; J. Fletcher/
OUP; FPG/S. Jones/GettyOne Telegraph; J. Franz/GettyOne Stone; Gordon
R. Gainer/corbisstockmarket.com; Mark E. Gibson; Michael Goldman/FPG;
Grantpix/Index Stock; S. Gray/OUP; A. Hall/Robert Harding Picture Library;
Kenneth Hamm/PhotoJapan; B. Handelman/GettyOne Stone; D. Hanover/
GettyOne Stone; P. Lee Harvey/GettyOne Stone; Chip Henderson/Index
Stock; John Henley/The Stockmarket; T. Henshaw/Action-Plus; E. Hesser/
GettyOne Telegraph; M. Hewitt/Action-Plus; T. Hill/Anthony Blake Photo
Library; Hollenbeck Photography/International Stock; Robert Holmes/
Corbis; Dave G. Houser/Corbis; HultonArchive/GettyOne Stone; Miwako
Ikeda/International Stock; ImageState; Index Stock; Index Stock/Powerstock
Zefa; IPS Company, Ltd./Index Stock; D. Jacobs/GettyOne Stone; I. Jones/
Gamma/Frank Spooner Pictures; Kaluzny/Thatcher/GettyOne Stone; Kim
Karpeles; David Katzenstein/Corbis; Michael Keller/The Stockmarket;
J. Kelly/GettyOne Stone; M. King/Action-Plus; G. Kirk/Action-Plus; G. Kirk/
Anthony Blake Photo Library; S. Kobayashi/GettyOne Stone; C. Kunin/
GettyOne Stone; Bill Lai/Index Stock; Catherine Ledner/Stone; M. Lewis/
GettyOne Stone; Lightscapes Inc./The Stockmarket; R. Lockyer/GettyOne
Image Bank; D. Madison/GettyOne Stone; T. Main/GettyOne Stone; Steve
Mason/PhotoDisc; Maximilian/Anthony Blake Photo Library; J. McLoughlin/
GettyOne Stone; Ryan McVay/PhotoDisc; B. Mitchell/GettyOne Image Bank;
P. Nicholson/GettyOne Telegraph; A. No/GettyOne Telegraph; Carlos Osorio/
Associated Press; Panoramic Images; Michael Paras/ImageState; D. Parker/
Science Photo Library; Jose Luis Pelaez Inc./corbisstockmarket.com; Photo-
Disc; PhotoDisc/Photomondo; Pictor International; Pictures Colour Library;
Todd Powell/Index Stock; J. Pumfrey/GettyOne Telegraph; RDL/Anthony
Blake Photo Library; H. Reinhard/Bruce Coleman Collection; C. Rennie/
Robert Harding Picture Library; Reuters New Media Inc./Corbis; Rex
Features; Mick Roessler/Index Stock; M. Rogers/GettyOne Stone; C. Rosenfeld/
GettyOne Stone; Samsung; D. Smetzer/GettyOne Stone; Joseph Sohm,
Chromo Sohm Inc./Corbis; Rick Stewart/Allsport; Superstock; Svobodastock/
ImageState; Chuck Szymanski/ImageState; Paul Thomson/ImageState;
N. Tingle/Action-Plus; Aldo Torelli/Stone; B. Torrez/GettyOne Stone;
J. Truchet/GettyOne Stone; R. Van Der Hilst/GettyOne Stone; VCL/GettyOne
Telegraph; Andrew Wakeford/PhotoDisc; John Walmsley; A. Weinbrecht/
GettyOne Stone; M. Westmorland/GettyOne Stone; Hilary Wilkes/ImageState;
Simon Wilkinson/The Image Bank; S. Williams/OUP; C. Windsor/GettyOne
Stone; F. Wing/GettyOne Stone; Caroline Wood/International Stock; John
Wood/Index Stock; J. Woodcock/Bubbles Photo Library; Jeff Zaruba/The
Stockmarket; Zefa Visual Media-Germany/Index Stock

Special thanks to: the Berkeley Carroll School, Brooklyn, NY; Canal Jeans;
Anthony Blake Photo Library, Courtesy of Apple (p. 6); Courtesy of the
Fairmont Banff Springs (p. 102); Courtesy of Alison Snow (p. 103); Yankees
Clubhouse Store

Location and studio photography by: Donatella Accardi/OUP, Gareth Boden,
Julie Fisher, Mark Mason, Stephen Ogilvy, Jodi Waxman/OUP

The publishers would also like to thank the following for their help:
p. 105 "THIS LAND IS YOUR LAND" Words and music by Woody
Guthrie. TRO-©Copyright 1956 (Renewed) 1958 (Renewed)1970 Ludlow
Music, Inc., New York, NY. Used by permission.

Contents

SCOPE AND SEQUENCE

v

1

Hi!

am/are/is · my/your · This is … · How are you? · What's this in English? · Numbers 1–10 · Plurals

STARTER

T 1.1 Say your name.

Hello. I'm Lisa.

Hi. I'm David.

WHAT'S YOUR NAME?

am / are / is, my / your

1 **T 1.2** Read and listen.

Sandra Hi. I'm Sandra. What's your name?
Kazu My name's Kazu.
Sandra Hi, Kazu.

T 1.2 Listen and repeat.

GRAMMAR SPOT

I'**m** = I am
name'**s** = name is
What'**s** = What is

2 Stand up and practice.

Hi. I'm _____.
What's your name?

My name's _____.

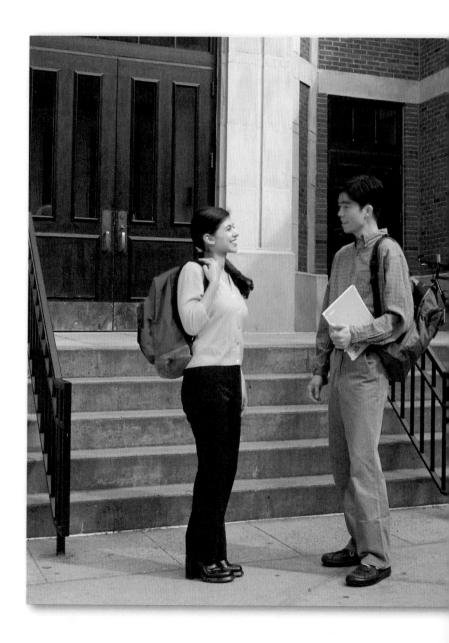

This is . . .

3 [T 1.3] Read and listen.

Sandra John, this is Kazu Shiga. Kazu, this is John Clark.
Kazu Hello, John.
John Hi, Kazu.

[T 1.3] Listen and repeat.

4 Practice in groups of three.

> _____, *this is* _____.
> _____, *this is* _____.

> *Hello,* _____.

> *Hi,* _____.

How are you?

5 **T 1.4** Read and listen.

Hi, John. How are you?

Fine, thanks, Sandra. And you?

I'm OK, thanks.

T 1.4 Listen and repeat.

6 **T 1.5** Read and listen.

Hi, Kazu. How are you?

Good, thanks. And you?

I'm fine, thanks.

T 1.5 Listen and repeat.

7 Answer your teacher.

Hi, _____. How are you?

Fine, thanks, _____. And you?

OK, thanks.

Fine, thanks.

Good, thanks.

8 Stand up and practice.

> **GRAMMAR SPOT**
>
> Write *am*, *is*, or *are*.
>
> I _____ Sandra.   How _____ you?   This _____ John.
>
> ▶▶ **Grammar Reference 1.1 and 1.2 p. 124**

PRACTICE

Introductions

1 Complete the conversations.

1. **A** Hello. ___My___ name's Anna.
   ___What's___ your name?
   B Ben.

2. **C** Hi. My _____ Carla.
   What's _____ name?
   D _____ name's Dennis.

   T 1.6 Listen and check. Practice the conversations.

2 Complete the conversations.

1. **B** _____, Anna. _____ are you?
   A Fine, thanks, Ben. _____ _____?
   B _____, thanks.

2. **D** Hi, Carla. _____ _____ you?
   C _____, thanks. _____ _____?
   D OK, _____.

   T 1.7 Listen and check. Practice the conversations.

3 **T 1.8** Listen and number the lines in the conversation.

☐ Fine, thanks.
☐ I'm OK, thanks. And you?
☐1☐ Hi. My name's Pam. What's your name?
☐ Hi, Tina. Hi, Mary.
☐ I'm Tina, and this is Mary.
☐ Hi, Pam. How are you?

T 1.8 Listen, check, and practice.

▶▶ **Grammar Reference 1.3 p. 124**

VOCABULARY
What's this in English?

1 Write the words.

a book	a camera	a car
a photograph	a computer	a bag
a hamburger	a television	
a sandwich	a house	

1 a photograph

2

3

4

5

6

7

8

9

10

2 [T 1.9] Listen and repeat the words.

3 [T 1.10] Listen and repeat.

> *What's this in English?*

> *It's a photograph.*

Work with a partner. Point to a picture. Ask and answer questions.

4 Go to things in the room. Ask your teacher.

> *What's this in English?*

EVERYDAY ENGLISH
Numbers 1–10 and plurals

1 **T 1.11** Read and listen. Practice the numbers.

1 one   **2** two   **3** three   **4** four   **5** five   **6** six   **7** seven   **8** eight   **9** nine   **10** ten

Say the numbers around the class.

2 Write the numbers.

a | ten | sandwiches

b | | books

c | | bags

d | | computers

e | | houses

f | | hamburgers

g | | cameras

h | | photographs

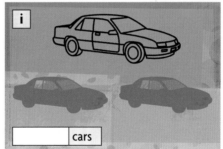
i | | cars

j | | students

T 1.12 Listen and check.

3 **T 1.13** Listen and repeat.

/s/	/z/	/ɪz/
books	cars	sandwiches
photographs	computers	houses
students	hamburgers	
	cameras	
	televisions	
	bags	

GRAMMAR SPOT

Singular	Plural
one book	two books
one sandwich	ten sandwiches

▶▶ **Grammar Reference 1.4 p. 124**

2 Your world

Countries · Where are you from? · *he/she/they* · *his/her* · Numbers 11–30

STARTER

1 Find the places on the map on p. 9. Find your country on the map.

Australia   Brazil   England   Taiwan   Korea   Mexico   Japan   Canada   the United States

2 **T 2.1** Listen and repeat.

WHERE ARE YOU FROM?
he/she, his/her

1 **T 2.2** Read and listen.

Kazu   Where are you from, Sandra?
Sandra   I'm from Mexico. Where are you from?
Kazu   I'm from Japan. From Tokyo.

T 2.2 Listen and repeat.

2 Where are you from? Stand up and practice.

3 **T 2.3** Read, listen, and repeat.

His name's Kazu. He's from Japan.

Her name's Sandra. She's from Mexico.

> **GRAMMAR SPOT**
>
> he's = he is   she's = she is
>
> ▶▶ **Grammar Reference 2.1 and 2.2 p. 124**

4 Complete the sentences.

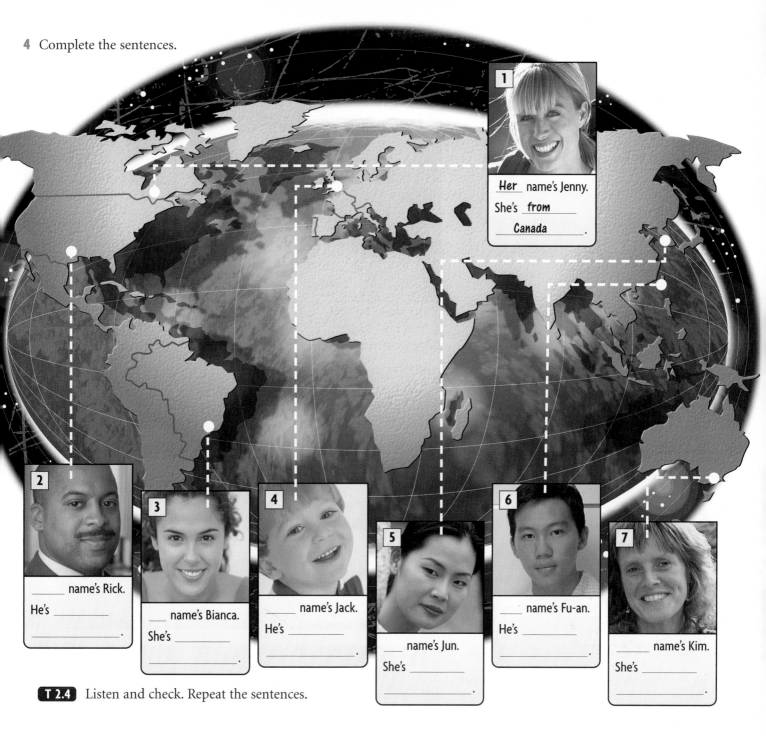

1

Her name's Jenny.
She's _from_
Canada .

2

_____ name's Rick.
He's _____
_____ .

3

___ name's Bianca.
She's _____
_____ .

4

_____ name's Jack.
He's _____
_____ .

5

_____ name's Jun.
She's _____
_____ .

6

___ name's Fu-an.
He's _____
_____ .

7

_____ name's Kim.
She's _____
_____ .

T 2.4 Listen and check. Repeat the sentences.

Questions

5 **T 2.5** Listen and repeat the questions.

What's his name?   Where's he from?
What's her name?   Where's she from?

6 Ask and answer questions about the people in the photographs.

What's his name?

His name's Kazu.

Where's he from?

He's from Japan.

GRAMMAR SPOT

1 Where**'s** = Where is
2 Complete the questions with _is_ or _are_.
   Where _____ she from?
   Where _____ he from?
   Where _____ you from?
   ▶▶ **Grammar Reference 2.3 p. 124**

PRACTICE

Cities and countries

1 Where are the cities? Ask and answer.

| Tokyo | Seoul | Toronto | Rio de Janeiro |
| London | Boston | Sydney | Mexico City |

Where's Tokyo?

It's in Japan.

T 2.6 Listen and check.

2 Work with a partner.

Student A Look at the photos on this page.
Student B Look at the photos on p. 108.

Ask questions and write the answers.

What's her name?

Where's he from?

Talking about you

3 Ask about the students in the class.

What's her name?

Her name's Ming-na.

Where's she from?

She's from Taiwan. From Taipei.

What's his name?

His name's Li-hong.

Where's he from?

He's from Taipei, too.

1

Her name's Mayumi.
She's from Tokyo.

2

_____
_____

4

_____
_____

6

_____
_____

7

His name's Ted.
He's from Boston.

10   Unit 2 · Your world

3

His name's Young-Soo.
He's from Seoul.

5

His name's Adam.
He's from Sydney.

8

_____

Questions and answers

4 **T 2.7** Listen and complete the conversation. Practice it.

S   Hi, I'm Sandra. What's
   your name?

L   _____ name's Luis.

S   Hi, Luis. Where are
   you _____?

L   _____ from Mexico.
   Where are _you_ from?

S   Oh, I'm from Mexico, too.
   _____ from Mexico City.

5 **T 2.8** Listen and write the countries.

1. Gabriel: **Brazil**_____
   Akemi: _____

2. Charles: _____
   Mike: _____

3. Loretta and Jason:

   _____

6 Match the questions and answers.

1. Where are you from?	His name's Luis.
2. What's her name?	He's from Mexico City.
3. What's his name?	It's in Canada.
4. Where's he from?	I'm from Brazil.
5. What's this in English?	Fine, thanks.
6. How are you?	Her name's Amina.
7. Where's Toronto?	It's a computer.

T 2.9 Listen and check.

Check it

7 Put a check next to (✓) the correct sentence.

1. ☐ My name Sandra.
   ✓ My name's Sandra.

2. ☐ What's he's name?
   ☐ What's his name?

3. ☐ "What's his name?" "Luis."
   ☐ "What's her name?" "Luis."

4. ☐ He's from Mexico.
   ☐ His from Mexico.

5. ☐ Where she from?
   ☐ Where's she from?

6. ☐ What's her name?
   ☐ What's she name?

Where are they from?

1 **T 2.10** Read and listen.

This is a photograph of Miguel and Angela da Costa from Rio de Janeiro. They are in New York. Miguel is from Brazil, and Angela is from Toronto in Canada. They are married. Miguel is a doctor. His hospital is in the center of Rio. Angela is a teacher. Her school is in the center of Rio, too.

2 Complete the sentences.
1. Miguel is from _____ .
2. He's a _____ .
3. His hospital is in the _____ of Rio.
4. Angela is from _____ in Canada.
5. She's a _____ .
6. Her _____ is in the center of Rio.
7. They _____ in New York.
8. They are _____ .

3 Write questions with *what* and *where* about Miguel and Angela. Ask a partner.

What/name? Where/from? Where/school? Where/hospital?

GRAMMAR SPOT

Write *is* or *are*.
He _____ a doctor.
She _____ a teacher.
They _____ from Brazil.
▶▶ **Grammar Reference 2.4 p. 124**

What's his name?

Where are they from?

EVERYDAY ENGLISH
Numbers 11–30

1 Say the numbers 1–10 around the class.

2 **T 2.11** Listen, read, and repeat.

11 eleven	12 twelve	13 thirteen	14 fourteen	15 fifteen
16 sixteen	17 seventeen	18 eighteen	19 nineteen	20 twenty

Say the numbers 1–20 around the class.

3 Match the numbers.

21   twenty-five
22   twenty-seven
23   twenty-one
24   twenty-eight
25   twenty-two
26   twenty-four
27   twenty-nine
28   twenty-three
29   thirty
30   twenty-six

T 2.12 Listen and repeat. Say the numbers 1–30 around the class.

4 **T 2.13** Listen and put a check next to (✓) the numbers you hear.

1. **22**   12 ✓   **10**   20
2. 17   15   16   14
3. 21   **29**   19   **9**
4. **11**   **7**   17   27
5. 23   **3**   13   30

5 Work with a partner.

Student A Write five numbers. Say them to your partner.
Student B Write the numbers you hear. *14 24 …*

3 Personal information

Jobs • *am/are/is* – negatives and questions • Address, phone number • Social expressions

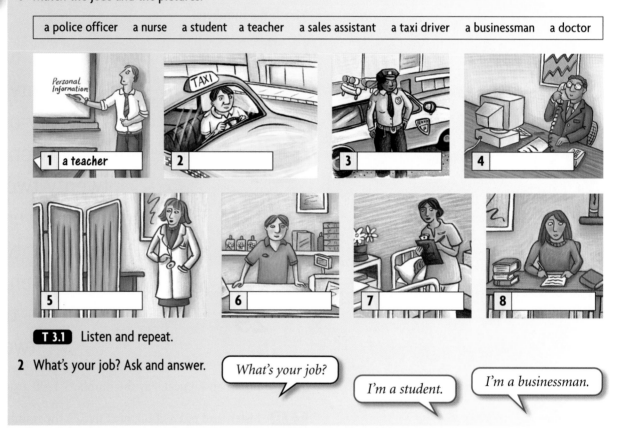

1 Match the jobs and the pictures.

> a police officer   a nurse   a student   a teacher   a sales assistant   a taxi driver   a businessman   a doctor

1	a teacher
2	
3	
4	
5	
6	
7	
8	

T 3.1 Listen and repeat.

2 What's your job? Ask and answer.

> *What's your job?*

> *I'm a student.*

> *I'm a businessman.*

WHAT'S HER JOB?
Negatives – *isn't*

1 **T 3.2** Listen and repeat.
What's his job? He's a teacher.
What's her job? She's a doctor.

Look at the pictures. Ask and answer questions with a partner.

2 **T 3.3** Listen and repeat.
He isn't a student. He's a teacher.
She isn't a nurse. She's a doctor.

Make more negative and affirmative sentences.

> *He/She isn't a _____ .*

> *He/She's a _____ .*

GRAMMAR SPOT

She **isn't** a nurse.	*isn't* = is not	This is negative.
He**'s a** teacher.	*'s* = is	This is affirmative.

---

14   Unit 3 · Personal information

Questions and short answers

3 Read the information.

fitness edge health club

FEHC

home
next>
<back
info

Name **Amy Roberts**
Country **United States**
Address **18 Cedar Street**
Chicago
Phone number **(773) 726-6049**
Age **20**
Job **Student**
Married? **No**

4 Complete the questions and answers.

1. What's her **name** ?   Amy Roberts.
2. Where's she _____ ?   The United States.
3. What's her _____ ?   18 Cedar Street, Chicago.
4. What's her _____ _____ ? It's (773) 726-6049.
5. How old is she?   She's _____ .
6. What's _____ _____ ?   _____ _____ _____ .
7. Is she _____ ?   No, she isn't.

T 3.4 Listen and check. Practice the questions and answers.

5 **T 3.5** Read and listen. Then listen and repeat.

Is Amy from England?   *No, she isn't.*   *Is she from Brazil?*   *Is she from the US?*

No, she isn't.   *Yes, she is.*

Ask and answer questions.

1. Is she from Portland? Dallas? Chicago?
2. Is she 16? 18? 20?
3. Is she a teacher? a nurse? a student?
4. Is she married?

6 Complete the sentences.

1. Amy **isn't** from England. She **'s** from the United States.
2. Her phone number _____ (763) 726-6049. It's (773) 726-6049.
3. She _____ 18. She _____ 20.
4. She _____ married.

> **GRAMMAR SPOT**
>
> Is she from the United States? Yes, **she is**.
> Is she married? No, **she isn't**.
> These are short answers.
> *Yes, she is (from the United States).*
> *No, she isn't (married).*

WHAT'S YOUR JOB?
Negatives and short answers

1 **T 3.6** Listen and complete the conversation.

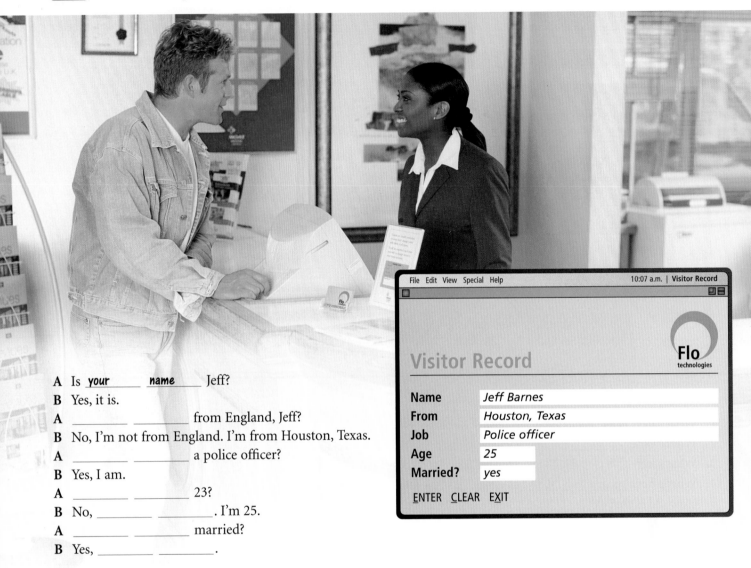

A Is _your_ _name_ Jeff?
B Yes, it is.
A _____ _____ from England, Jeff?
B No, I'm not from England. I'm from Houston, Texas.
A _____ _____ a police officer?
B Yes, I am.
A _____ _____ 23?
B No, _____ _____. I'm 25.
A _____ _____ married?
B Yes, _____ _____.

File Edit View Special Help   10:07 a.m. | Visitor Record

Visitor Record   **Flo** technologies

Name	Jeff Barnes
From	Houston, Texas
Job	Police officer
Age	25
Married?	yes

ENTER CLEAR EXIT

T 3.6 Listen again and check.

GRAMMAR SPOT

1 **I'm not** from England. *I'm not* = I am not
   This is negative.
2 Yes, **I am**. No, **I'm not**.   Yes, **it is**. No, **it isn't**.
   These are short answers.

▶▶ **Grammar Reference 3.1 p. 125**

---

2 Answer your teacher.

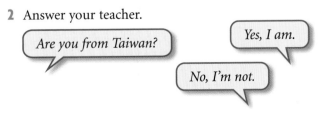

Are you from Taiwan?

Yes, I am.

No, I'm not.

3 Stand up. Ask and answer questions.

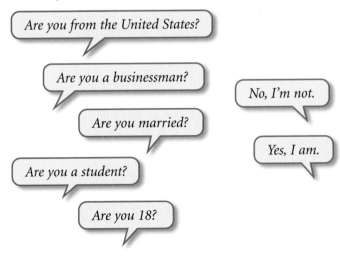

Are you from the United States?

Are you a businessman?

Are you married?

Are you a student?

Are you 18?

No, I'm not.

Yes, I am.

PRACTICE

Listening and speaking

1 **T 3.7** Listen to the conversations. Complete the chart.

Name	Sang-hoon Pak	Diana Black
Country	Korea	
City/town		
Phone number		(646) 463-9145
Age	23	
Job		sales assistant
Married?	No	

Diana

Sang-hoon Pak

T 3.7 Listen again and check.

2 Ask and answer the questions with a partner. Use short answers.

Is Sang-hoon from Seoul?
Is he a nurse?
Is his phone number (822) 773-3862?

Is Diana from the United States?
Is she a teacher?
Is she 29?

Talking about you

3 Complete the questions.

1. <u>What's</u> <u>your</u> name?
2. _____ _____ you from?
3. _____ _____ phone number?
4. How old _____ _____ ?
5. _____ _____ job?
6. _____ _____ married?

In groups, ask and answer the same questions.

4 Write about one student.

Her name's Yaling. She's from Taiwan. Her phone number is …

Check it

5 Put a check (✓) next to the correct sentence.

1. ☐ She's name's Soraya.
   ☐ Her name's Soraya.
2. ☐ Her job is teacher.
   ☐ She's a teacher.
3. ☐ Are you from Brazil?
   ☐ Is you from Brazil?
4. ☐ He's phone number is 796-5242.
   ☐ His phone number is 796-5242.
5. ☐ How old is she?
   ☐ How old she is?
6. ☐ She is no married.
   ☐ She isn't married.
7. ☐ "Are you married?" "Yes, I'm."
   ☐ "Are you married?" "Yes, I am."

1 Read about the pop group 4x4.

This is the pop group **4x4** (Four by Four). Melanie Ryan is from Australia. Robert Lacoste is from Canada. Jennifer and Jason Walters are from the United States. They're on tour in the US.

"We're in New York. We're at Radio City Music Hall. It's great!" Who is married in 4x4? Robert: "I'm not married." Jason and Jennifer: "We aren't married!" Melanie: "I am!"

2 Complete the sentences.

1. The name of the group __is__ __4x4__ .
2. _____ _____ _____ from Australia.
3. Jennifer and Jason Walters _____ _____ the United States.
4. _____ _____ _____ _____ Canada.
5. "We _____ on tour in the United States."

3 **T 3.8** Listen and answer the questions.

1. How old is Melanie?
2. How old are Jennifer and Jason?
3. How old is Robert?
4. Who's married? Who isn't married?

GRAMMAR SPOT

We**'re** in New York. *we're* = we are

We **aren't** married. *we aren't* = we are not
This is negative.

▶▶ **Grammar Reference 3.2 p. 125**

4 Work in groups of four. You are a pop group.

- What are your names?
- What's the name of your group?
- How old are you?
- Where are you now?
- Where are you from?

Ask and answer questions with another group.

EVERYDAY ENGLISH
Social expressions

1 Complete the conversations. Use these words.

Good afternoon	Good night	Good morning	Good-bye

A <u>Good</u> <u>morning</u> .
B _____ _____ ,
Mr. Brown.

A _____ _____ .
The Grand Hotel.
B _____ _____ .

A _____ _____ .
B _____ _____ ,
Peter.

A _____ !
B _____ ! Have
a good trip!

T 3.9 Listen and check. Practice the conversations.

2 **T 3.10** Listen and complete the conversations. Use these words.

excuse me	don't understand	don't know	sorry	thank you

1. **A** What's this in English?
   B I <u>don't</u> <u>know</u> .
   A It's a dictionary.

2. **A** *Hogy hívnak?*
   B _____ . I _____ _____ .
   A What's your name?
   B My name's Manuel. I'm from
   Venezuela.

3. **A** The homework is on page …
   of the Workbook.
   B _____ _____ ?
   A The homework is on page *30*
   of the Workbook.
   B _____ _____ .

3 Practice the conversations.

4 Family and friends

our/their • Possessive *'s* • Family relations • *has/have* • The alphabet • On the phone

STARTER

1 Complete the chart.

Subject pronoun	I	you	he	she	we	they
Possessive adjective	*my*				*our*	*their*

T 4.1 Listen and check.

2 Talk about things in the classroom.

This is my book.

This is our class.

This is her bag.

PATTY'S FAMILY

Possessive *'s* – family relations

1 **T 4.2** Read and listen.

This is Patty Milton.

She's married, and this is her family. Their house is in Los Angeles. She's a teacher. Her school is in the center of town.

Tom is Patty's husband. He's a bank manager. His bank is in the center of town, too.

"Our children are Kayla and Nick. They're students at Hollywood High School. We're happy in Los Angeles."

2 Answer the questions.

1. Is Patty married?   *Yes, she is.*
2. Where's their house?   _____
3. What is Patty's job?   _____
4. Where's her school?   _____
5. What is Tom's job?   _____
6. Where's his bank?   _____
7. Are their children doctors? _____

T 4.3 Listen and check.

3 **T 4.4** Listen and repeat.

♀	mother	daughter	sister	wife
♂	father	son	brother	husband

Plural	parents	children

4 **T 4.5** Look at the family tree. Listen and complete the sentences.

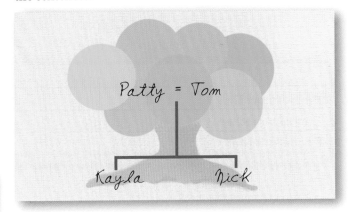

Patty = Tom
Kayla   Nick

1. Patty is Tom's **wife**.
2. Tom is Patty's _____.
3. Kayla is Patty and Tom's _____.
4. Nick is their _____.
5. Patty is Nick's _____.
6. Tom is Kayla's _____.
7. Kayla is Nick's _____.
8. Nick is Kayla's _____.
9. Patty and Tom are Kayla and Nick's _____.
10. Kayla and Nick are Tom and Patty's _____.

T 4.5 Listen and check.

5 Ask and answer questions.

Who's Nick?

He's Kayla's brother.

He's Tom's son.

This is our house.

Kayla and Nick's school

PRACTICE

The family

1 **T 4.6** Listen to Rachel Choi. Complete the information about her family.

	Name	Age	Job
Rachel's brother			
Rachel's mother			
Rachel's father			

2 Complete the sentences.

1. Steve is **Rachel's** brother.
2. Her _____ name is Grace.
3. Grace is Joe's _____.
4. "What's _____ job?" "He's a businessman."
5. "Where's _____ house?" "It's in San Diego."

3 Write the names of your family. Ask and answer questions with a partner.

Toshi   Kumiko

Who's Toshi/Kumiko?

He's/She's my brother/mother …

How old is he/she?

He's/She's _____.

What's his/her job?

He's/She's a _____.

my/our/your . . .

4 Complete the sentences with a possessive adjective.

1. "What's **your** name?"
   "My name's Patty."
2. "What are _____ names?"
   "Our names are Kayla and Nick."
3. Daniel and Marta are students.
   _____ school is in Mexico City.
4. "My sister's married."
   "What's _____ husband's name?"
5. "My brother's office is in New York."
   "What's _____ job?"
6. We are in _____ English class.
7. "Mom and Dad are in Seattle."
   "What's _____ phone number?"

PATTY'S BROTHER
has/have

1 **T 4.7** Read and listen to David.

This is David Simpson and his family.

"We're from Vermont. I have a small farm. My wife's name is Megan, and she has a job in town. She's a sales assistant. We have one child, Brian, and two dogs, Dylan and Dolly.

My sister, Patty, and her husband, Tom, have a big house in Los Angeles. They have two children. Tom has a very good job."

2 Are the sentences true (✔) or false (✗)?
1. ☐ David's farm is in Vermont.
2. ☐ David is Patty's brother.
3. ☐ His wife has a job in a hospital.
4. ☐ David and Megan have two children.
5. ☐ Their farm is big.
6. ☐ They have two dogs, Brian and Dolly.

3 **T 4.8** Listen and write the sentences. Practice them.
1. I have a small farm in Vermont.
2. _____
3. _____
4. _____
5. _____
6. _____
7. _____

GRAMMAR SPOT

Complete the forms of the verb *have*.

I	_____
You	have
He	has
She	_____
We	_____
They	_____

▶▶ Grammar Reference 4.4 p. 126

4 Write sentences about your family. Tell the class.

I have two sisters.

We have a house in the country.

PRACTICE

has/have

1 Complete the sentences. Use *has* or *have*.

1. I **have** two brothers and a sister.
2. My parents _____ a house in the country.
3. My wife _____ a Japanese car.
4. My sister and I _____ a dog.
5. You _____ a very nice family.
6. Our school _____ 15 classrooms.
7. We _____ English classes in the evening.

2 Talk about your school.

> *Our school is small.*

> *It has six classrooms.*

> *We have ten students in our class.*

Questions and answers

3 Match the questions and answers.

1. How is your mother?	Yes, we are.
2. What's your sister's job?	She's David's sister.
3. How old are your brothers?	It's in the center of town.
4. Who is Patty?	She's fine, thank you.
5. Where's your office?	They're ten and thirteen.
6. Are you and your husband from Peru?	She's a nurse.

T 4.9 Listen and check.

Check it

4 Put a check (✓) next to the correct sentence.

1. ☐ Mary's children are married.
   ☐ Mary is children are married.
2. ☐ What's your daughter name?
   ☐ What's your daughter's name?
3. ☐ What's he's job?
   ☐ What's his job?
4. ☐ They're from Thailand.
   ☐ Their from Thailand.
5. ☐ They're parents have a house in Bangkok.
   ☐ Their parents have a house in Bangkok.
6. ☐ My brother have a good job.
   ☐ My brother has a good job.
7. ☐ We house is in the center of town.
   ☐ Our house is in the center of town.

READING AND WRITING
My best friend

1 Read about Andy. Check the new words in your dictionary.

2 Match the photographs with a part of the text.

My friend Andy

a My **best friend**'s name is Andy. He's **very nice**, and he's **really funny**. He's 22, and he's a **college** student. He isn't married, **but** he has a **beautiful girlfriend**. Her name is Carrie, and she's Canadian.

b Andy's parents have a **house** in Brooklyn. His father's a police officer, and his mother has a **part-time** job in a hospital.

c He has two sisters. Their names are Allison and Mary Ann. They're **both** in school.

d Andy has **a lot of CDs**. His **favorite music** is rock 'n roll, and his favorite **group** is Mood. He is **also** a **fan** of the New York Yankees!

When we're **together**, we **have a good time**.

1 **a**

3

3 Underline the correct information.

1. Andy is … <u>a student</u> / a bus driver / Canadian / <u>nice</u> / <u>funny</u> / beautiful.
2. Andy has … two sisters / two brothers / a wife / a girlfriend / a lot of CDs.
3. Carrie is … Andy's sister / Andy's girlfriend / Canadian / beautiful.
4. Andy's parents have … a house / an apartment / one daughter / three children.
5. Andy is … in a group called Mood / a fan of Mood / a fan of the New York Yankees.

4 Work with a partner. Talk about Andy.

> *Andy's a student. He's very …*

5 Write about a good friend.

- My friend's name is …
- She's/He's …
- She/He has …
- Her/His parents …
- Her/His favorite …

Write about family, job, favorite music/sport …

The alphabet

1 **T 4.10** Listen to the letters of the alphabet. Practice them.

A B C D
E F G H I J K
L M N O P
Q R S T U V W X Y Z

2 Practice the letters in groups.

/eɪ/	a h j k	/oʊ/	o
/i/	b c d e g p t v z	/u/	q u w
/ɛ/	f l m n s x	/ɑ/	r
/aɪ/	i y		

3 **T 4.11** Listen to people spell their first name (Patty) and their last name (Milton). Write the names.

1. Patty   Milton
2. _____ _____
3. _____ _____
4. _____ _____
5. _____ _____

4 Practice spelling your name with a partner.

> *How do you spell your first name?*

> *M - a - r - i - s - o - l.*

> *How do you spell your last name?*   *D - i - a - z.*

5 In pairs, ask and answer *How do you spell …?* with words from the text about Andy on p. 24.

> *How do you spell "friend"?*   *F - r - i - e - n - d.*

6 Put the letters in the correct order. What's the country?

1. O E K R A   Korea
2. A N A A C D _____
3. L A R Z I B _____
4. N A P A J _____
5. L A S A R U T A I _____
6. X E M C O I _____
7. G A N E L D N _____

On the phone

7 **T 4.12** Listen to the phone conversations.

1. **A** Good morning. The Grand Hotel.
   B Hello. Can I speak to the manager, please?
   A Certainly. Who's calling, please?
   B Luis Gonzalez.
   A How do you spell your last name?
   B G – o – n – z – a – l – e – z.
   A Thank you.
   C Hello. Sam Jackson.
   B Hello, Mr. Jackson. This is Luis Gonzalez …

2. **D** Good afternoon. Springfield English School.
   E Hello. Can I speak to the director, Ann Benton, please?
   D Who's calling, please?
   E Mayumi Okano.
   D M – a …
   E M – a – y – u – m – i   O – k – a – n – o.
   D Thank you. I'm sorry. She isn't in her office. What's your phone number?
   E In Japan. It's 3-5414-6443.
   D Thank you for calling. Good-bye.
   E Good-bye.

soac

calle Santiago 5, 1003 Buenos Aires
tel 54-11-4782-1156 fax 54-11-4782-1106

Señor Luis Gonzalez
export manager

tanko design

2-21-10 #204 Akasaka Building
Sendagaya Shibuya-ku
Tokyo 1510051 JAPAN

phone/+81-3-5414-6443
fax/+81-3-5414-6443
e-mail/mokano@tanko.co.jp
http://www.tanko.co.jp

Mayumi Okano

8 Write your business card. Have similar phone conversations.

company name

your name

address

phone number   fax number

e-mail

5 It's my life!

Sports, food, and drinks · Present Simple – *I/you/they* · *a /an* · Languages and nationalities
Numbers and prices

1 Match the words and pictures.

Sports	Food	Drinks
1 tennis	Italian food	tea
basketball	Chinese food	coffee
swimming	pizza	soda
skiing	hamburgers	juice
	oranges	water
	ice cream	

T 5.1 Listen and repeat.

2 Put a check (✓) next to the things you like. 😀 Put an (✗) next to the things you don't like. 😠

THINGS I LIKE

Present Simple–*I / you*

1 **T 5.2** Listen and repeat.

I like tennis. I don't like basketball.

I like pizza. I don't like hamburgers.

2 **T 5.3** Listen to Bill. Complete the sentences.

I like **swimming** , _____, _____, _____, _____, _____, and _____.

3 Talk to a partner about the sports, food, and drinks on p. 28.

I like tennis, but I don't like basketball.

Questions

4 **T 5.4** Listen and repeat.

Do you like tennis?
Yes, I do.

Do you like basketball?
No, I don't.

5 Ask your teacher about the sports, food, and drinks.

Do you like swimming?

Do you like Italian food?

6 Ask and answer the questions with a partner.

Do you like tennis?

Yes, I do. Do **you** like tennis?

No, I don't.

Bill

PRACTICE

Reading and listening

1 **T 5.5** Read and listen to the text.

BRAD WILSON
from Cleveland

" Hi! My name's Brad Wilson. I come from Cleveland in Ohio, but now I live and work in New York City. I have a very small apartment downtown. I'm a waiter and I'm also a drama student. I work in an Italian restaurant. I eat Italian and Mexican food. I drink coffee, but I don't drink tea. I don't like it. And I don't play sports. I speak three languages—English, Spanish, and a little French. I want to be an actor. "

GRAMMAR SPOT

a small apartment	**an** actor
a waiter	**an I**talian restaurant

▶▶ **Grammar Reference 5.1 and 5.2 p. 126**

---

2 **T 5.6** Listen and repeat the questions.

Questions	Answers
1. Do you come from Ohio?	Yes, I _do_____.
2. Do you live in Cleveland?	No, I _don't_____. I _____ in New York.
3. Do you live in an apartment?	Yes, I _____. I _____ in an apartment downtown.
4. Do you work in a Chinese restaurant?	No, I _____. I _____ in an Italian restaurant.
5. Do you like Italian food?	Yes, I _____. I _____ it a lot.
6. Do you like your job?	No, I _____. I want to be _____ _____.
7. Do you drink tea?	No, I _____. I _____ like it.
8. Do you speak Spanish and German?	I _____ Spanish, but I _____ speak German.

T 5.7 Listen and complete the conversation.

3 Ask and answer the questions with a partner. Give true answers.

Talking about you

4 **T 5.8** Listen and repeat the questions. Write about you.

1. Where do you live? (house or apartment?)	I live in a/an _____.
2. What do you do?	I'm a/an _____.
3. Where do you work?	I work in _____.
4. What sports do you like?	I like _____.
5. What drinks do you like?	I like _____.
6. How many languages do you speak?	I speak ___ languages— _____ _____.

Ask and answer the questions with a partner.

Role play

5 Work with a partner.
   Student A Go to page 109.
   Student B Go to page 110.

Check it

6 Put a check (✓) next to the correct sentence.

1. ☐ Live you in Osaka?
   ☐ Do you live in Osaka?

2. ☐ Where do you come from?
   ☐ Where you come from?

3. ☐ Do you speak Chinese?
   ☐ Are you speak Chinese?

4. ☐ I don't speak Chinese.
   ☐ I no speak Chinese.

5. ☐ "Do you like basketball?" "Yes, I like."
   ☐ "Do you like basketball?" "Yes, I do."

6. ☐ "Are you married?" "No, I don't."
   ☐ "Are you married?" "No, I'm not."

7. ☐ He's a actor.
   ☐ He's an actor.

VOCABULARY AND PRONUNCIATION
Languages and nationalities

1 Match the countries and nationalities.

T 5.9 Listen, check, and repeat.

England	Japanese
Italy	French
Spain	Korean
Mexico	Chinese
Brazil	Spanish
Japan	Brazilian
China	Mexican
France	Italian
the United States	American
Korea	English

2 What nationality are the people in the pictures, do you think?

> *I think they're English.*

> *I think they're American.*

3 Make true sentences.

1. In Brazil		Korean.
2. In Canada		Italian.
3. In France		Japanese.
4. In England		Portuguese.
5. In Italy		Spanish.
6. In Japan	they speak	English.
7. In Mexico		French.
8. In Taiwan		Chinese.
9. In Spain		
10. In Korea		
11. In the United States		

T 5.10 Listen and check.

4 Practice the question. Ask and answer questions with a partner.

> *What do they speak in Brazil?*

> *Portuguese.*

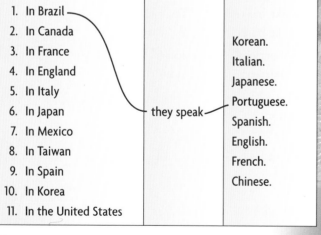
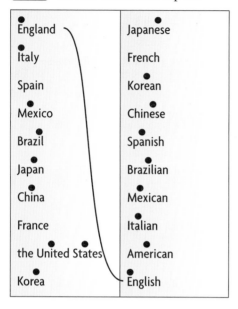

5 Write the nationality.

1 an American car

2 a Korean TV

3 oranges

4 a camera

5 food

6 an dictionary

7 an bag

8 coffee

9 tea

T 5.11 Listen and check.

▶▶ **Grammar Reference 5.3 p. 126**

6 Write sentences about you. Use the verbs *have*, *eat*, and *drink*.
   I drink Brazilian coffee, but I don't drink Chinese tea.

7 Write questions. Ask and answer with a partner.

Do you have an American car?

Yes, I do.

No, I don't. I have a Japanese car.

Do you drink Chinese tea?

Yes, I do.

No, I don't. I don't drink tea. I don't like it.

LISTENING AND SPEAKING

At a party

1 **T 5.12** Justin and Alessandra are at a party in Seattle.
Listen to the conversation. Put a check (✔) next to what Justin says.

1. ✔ I work in Seattle.
   ☐ I don't work in Seattle.
2. ☐ I live in Seattle.
   ☐ I live in Tacoma.
3. ☐ I'm an actor.
   ☐ I'm a doctor.
4. ☐ You don't speak English very well.
   ☐ You speak English very well.
5. ☐ I like Brazil.
   ☐ I love Brazil.
6. ☐ I like the people and the food a lot.
   ☐ I don't like the people and the food a lot.

2 Practice the conversation. Look at the tapescript on p. 118.

Role play

3 You are at a party in Seattle. Think of a new identity.
Complete the role card.

Name:	Job:
Work in:	Live in:
Speak:	Like:

Hi. I'm _____.

Hi. I'm _____.

Do you live here?

4 Stand up. Talk to people at the party.

EVERYDAY ENGLISH

Numbers and prices

1 Count from 1–30 around the class.

2 🔊 **T 5.13** Listen and repeat.

10 ten
20 twenty
30 thirty
40 forty
50 fifty
60 sixty
70 seventy
80 eighty
90 ninety
100 one hundred

Count to 100 in tens around the class.

3 Work with a partner.

Student A
Write some numbers.
Say them to your partner.

thirty-two   *forty-five*

Student B
Write the numbers you hear.
32 45 …

4 🔊 **T 5.14** Read and listen to the prices.
Practice them.

30¢	thirty cents
50¢	fifty cents
75¢	seventy-five cents
$1	one dollar
$20	twenty dollars
$75	seventy-five dollars
$1.60	a dollar sixty
$3.45	three forty-five
$22.80	twenty-two eighty

5 Say the prices.

60¢	97¢	$17	$70	$25
$1.50	$16.80	$40.75	$26.99	

🔊 **T 5.15** Listen and check.

6 🔊 **T 5.16** Listen and put a check (✓) next to the prices you hear.

1 chicken sandwich
$3.19 ☐
$3.90 ✓

2 BASEBALL
$14 ☐
$40 ☐

3 Camera $19.99 ☐
$90.99 ☐

4 •WATER•
$1.15 ☐
$1.50 ☐

5 CHOCOLATE
50¢ ☐ 60¢ ☐

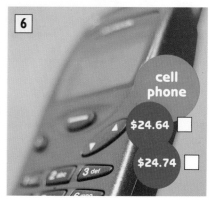

6 cell phone
$24.64 ☐
$24.74 ☐

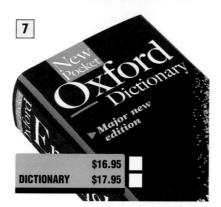

7 Oxford Dictionary
$16.95 ☐
DICTIONARY $17.95 ☐

8 bag
$13.99 ☐
$30.99 ☐

7 Ask and answer questions about the pictures with a partner.

How much is the chicken sandwich?

It's $3.90.

6 Every day

STARTER

1 **T 6.1** Listen and repeat. Write the times.

1. It's nine o'clock.   4. It's ten o'clock.   7. It's _____.   10. It's _____.
2. It's nine thirty.   5. It's ten fifteen.   8. It's _____.
3. It's nine forty-five.   6. It's _____.   9. It's _____.

2 **T 6.2** Listen to the conversation.

A What time is it, please?
B It's nine o'clock.
A Thank you.

Work with a partner. Ask and answer questions about the clocks.

WHAT TIME DO YOU . . . ?
Present Simple – *I/you*

1 **T 6.3** Listen to Lena talking about her weekdays.
Circle the times she says.

1 I get up at 7:30 / 7:45.

2 I have breakfast at 8:00 / 8:15.

3 I go to school at 8:30 / 8:40.

4 I have lunch at 12:15 / 12:45.

5 I leave school at 3:30 / 4:00.

6 I get home at 4:30 / 4:45.

7 I go to bed at 11:00 / 11:30.

T 6.3 Listen and check. Practice the sentences.

2 Talk to a partner about your day.

> *I get up at seven thirty. I have breakfast at …*

3 **T 6.4** Listen and repeat the questions.
What time do you get up?
What time do you have breakfast?

Work with another partner. Ask and answer questions about your day.

> *What time do you go to work?*

> *I go to work at 8:15.*

KEN'S DAY

Present Simple – *he / she / it,*
usually / sometimes / never

1 Ken Williams is 22 and he is a computer
millionaire. He's the director of
netstore24-7.com, a 24-hour shopping
site on the Internet.

Read about his day. Write the times.

1. He gets up at *six o'clock* and he
   takes a shower.

2. He has breakfast at _____.

3. He leaves home at _____ and he goes
   to work by taxi.

4. He has lunch (a soda and a sandwich) in his
   office at _____.

5. He usually works late. He leaves work at
   _____ in the evening.

6. He sometimes buys a pizza and eats it at
   home. He gets home at _____.

7. He never goes out in the evening. He works
   on his computer from _____ to
   _____.

8. He goes to bed at _____.

GRAMMAR SPOT

1 Underline the verbs in 1–8.
   gets up   *takes*
   What is the last letter?
   T 6.5 Listen and repeat.

2 Look at the adverbs of frequency.

90% usually	40% sometimes	0% never

   Find *usually, sometimes, never* in 1–8.
   T 6.6 Listen and repeat.
   ►► **Grammar Reference 6.1–6.3 p. 127**

6:00 AM

6:45 AM

1:00 PM

8:00 PM

9:30 PM

11:30 PM

7:15 AM

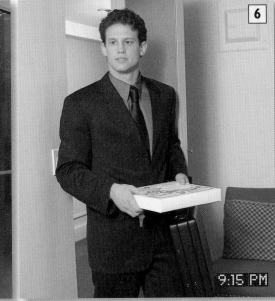

9:15 PM

11:45 PM

Questions and negatives

2 Read the questions. Complete the answers.

1.	What time does he get up?	He _____ up at 6:00.
2.	When does he go to bed?	He _____ to bed at 11:45.
3.	Does he go to work by taxi?	_____, he does.
4.	Does he have lunch in a restaurant?	_____, he doesn't.
5.	Does he go out in the evening?	No, he _____.

T 6.7 Listen, check, and repeat. Practice the questions and answers.

GRAMMAR SPOT

1   He get**s** up early.
What time **does** he get up?
       He **doesn't** get up late.   *doesn't* = does not

2   Does he get up early?   Yes, he does.
Does he have lunch at home?   No, he doesn't.
                                       These are short answers.

---

3 Work with a partner. Ask and answer questions about Ken's day.

> *What time does he have breakfast?*

> *He has breakfast at 6:45.*

Ask and answer about these things.

1. What time/have breakfast?
2. When/leave home?
3. Does/go to work by bus?
4. Where/have lunch?
5. Does/usually work late?
6. Does/eat in a restaurant?
7. What/do in the evening?

T 6.8 Listen and check.

GRAMMAR SPOT

1 Complete the chart for the Present Simple.

	Affirmative	Negative
I	work	don't work
You		
He		
She	works	doesn't work
We		
They		

2 Complete the questions.

1. When _____ you get up?   2. When _____ he get up?

▶▶ **Grammar Reference 6.4 p. 127**

---

4 Work with a partner.
Student A   Go to page 109.
Student B   Go to page 110.

PRACTICE

Katya's day

1 Ken has a sister, Katya. Her day is different. Complete the text with the verbs.

gets	gets up (x2)	has	paints	drinks
cooks	listens to	goes (x2)	plays	lives

Katya is 25. She's an artist.

She _lives_ in a small house in the country. She usually _____ at ten o'clock in the morning. She never _____ early. She _____ coffee and toast for breakfast and then she _____ for a walk with her dog. She _____ home at eleven o'clock and she _____ in her studio until seven o'clock in the evening. Then she _____ dinner and _____ a cup of tea. After dinner, she sometimes _____ music and she sometimes _____ the piano. She usually _____ to bed very late, at one or two o'clock in the morning.

T 6.9 Listen and check.

2 Is the sentence about Ken or Katya? Write *he* or *she*.

1. _He_ 's a millionaire.
2. _She_ 's an artist.
3. _____ lives in the country.
4. _____ doesn't have a dog.
5. _____ gets up very early.
6. _____ works at home in a studio.
7. _____ doesn't work in an office.
8. _____ doesn't cook.
9. _____ likes tea.
10. _____ loves computers.

Practice the sentences.

Negatives and pronunciation

3 Correct the sentences about Katya and Ken.

1. She lives in the city.

   She doesn't live in the city. She lives in the country.

2. He gets up at ten o'clock.

   _____

3. She has a big breakfast.

   _____

4. He has a dog.

   _____

5. She works in an office.

   _____

6. He cooks dinner in the evening.

   _____

7. She goes to bed early.

   _____

8. They go out in the evening.

   _____

T 6.10 Listen, check, and repeat.

Talking about you

4 Work with a partner. Write the names of two people in your family. Ask and answer questions about them.

- Who is . . . ?
- How old is . . . ?
- What does . . . do?
- Where does . . . live?
- Where does . . . work?
- What time does she/he . . . ?
- Does she/he have . . . ?

Maria

Alfonso

Who is she?   She's my sister.

Who is he?   He's my grandfather.

Check it

5 Complete the questions and answers with _do_, _don't_, _does_, or _doesn't_.

1. "_____ you like ice cream?"   "Yes, I _____."
2. "_____ she work in Dallas?"   "Yes, she _____."
3. "Where _____ he work?"   "In a bank."
4. "_____ you go to work by bus?"   "No, I _____."
5. "_____ she go to bed early?"   "No, she _____."
6. "_____ they have a dog?"   "Yes, they _____."
7. "_____ he speak Japanese?"   "No, he _____."
8. "_____ they live in England?"   "No, they _____."

VOCABULARY AND SPEAKING

Words that go together

1 Match a verb in **A** with a line in **B**.

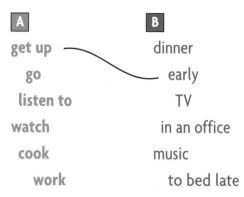

A	**B**
get up	dinner
go	early
listen to	TV
watch	in an office
cook	music
work	to bed late

A	**B**
go	in restaurants
take	the piano
eat	water
drink	shopping
play	home
stay	a shower

T 6.11 Listen and check.

2 **T 6.12** Look at the questionnaire. Listen and practice the questions.

3 Ask a partner the questions and complete the questionnaire. Put a check (✓) in the correct column.

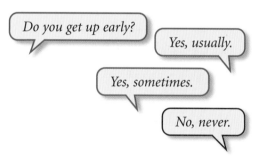

Do you get up early?

Yes, usually.

Yes, sometimes.

No, never.

4 Tell the class about you and your partner.

*Luis usually gets up early.
I never get up early.*

lifestyle
QUESTIONNAIRE

Do you ... ?

		USUALLY	SOMETIMES	NEVER
1	get up early	☐	☐	☐
2	have a big breakfast	☐	☐	☐
3	walk to school/work	☐	☐	☐
4	go to school/work by bus	☐	☐	☐
5	watch TV in the evening	☐	☐	☐
6	go shopping on the weekend	☐	☐	☐
7	eat in restaurants	☐	☐	☐
8	drink coffee	☐	☐	☐
9	go to bed late	☐	☐	☐

EVERYDAY ENGLISH
Days of the week

1 **T 6.13** Listen and put the days in order.

Wednesday	Friday	Tuesday	Saturday	Thursday

1 Monday	**2** ___	**3** ___	**4** ___	**5** ___	**6** ___	**7** Sunday

T 6.13 Listen again and repeat. Practice the days.

2 Answer the questions.
1. What day is it today?
2. What day is it tomorrow?
3. What days do you go to school/work?
4. What days are the weekend?
5. What days do you like?
6. What days don't you like?

3 Write the correct preposition in the boxes.

in	on	at

Sunday

Monday

Saturday evening

Thursday morning

Friday afternoon

the weekend

nine o'clock

ten thirty

twelve fifteen

the morning

the afternoon

the evening

T 6.14 Listen and check.

4 Write the correct preposition. Then answer the questions.

Do you have English class . . .
1. _____ nine o'clock?
2. _____ Sunday?
3. _____ the evening?
4. _____ Monday morning?
5. _____ the weekend?

When do you have English class?

Yes, we do.

No, we don't.

We have English class . . .

5 Ask and answer questions with a partner.

Do you . . .
- take a shower . . . the morning/evening?
- get up early . . . Sunday morning?
- go to work/school . . . Saturday?
- eat in restaurants . . . the weekend?
- watch TV . . . the afternoon?
- stay home . . . Friday evening?

Unit 6 · Every day   43

7 Places I like

Question words · *it/them* · *this/that* · Adjectives · Can I ... ?

STARTER

1 Match the questions and answers.

A	B
1. What is the capital of Australia?	4,500 years old.
2. How old are the Pyramids?	Eighty-six.
3. What time do Mexican people have dinner?	$3.50.
4. Where does the American president live?	The queen of England.
5. How many floors does the Empire State Building have?	In the White House.
6. How much is a hamburger in the US?	Canberra.
7. Who lives in Buckingham Palace?	Late. At 9:00 in the evening.

T 7.1 Listen and check.

2 What is your favorite town or city? Why do you like it?

I LOVE IT HERE!

it/them, this/that

1 **T 7.2** Listen and complete the conversation on p. 45. Use these words.

> why   because   me   you   him   it   them

2 Practice the conversation with a partner.

3 Complete the questions and answers.

1. Why __does__ Celine live in London?   Because she _____ it in England.
2. Does she like English people?   Yes, she loves _____ .
3. How _____ children does she have?   Three.
4. Where _____ her sons go to school?   In England.
5. _____ does Lisa-Marie go to school in the US?   _____ she lives with her father.

GRAMMAR SPOT

1 Underline the question words in the *Starter*.   *What*   *How old*

2 Complete the chart.

Subject pronoun	I	you	he	she	it	we	they
Object pronoun				her		us	

3 Find examples of *this* and *that* in the conversation with Celine.

▶▶ **Grammar Reference 7.1–7.3 p. 127**

CELINE, THE FAMOUS HOLLYWOOD MOVIE STAR, IS IN HER HOUSE IN LONDON. SHE IS WITH GARY NORMAN, A JOURNALIST.

Gary: This is a very beautiful house.

Celine: Thank you. I like it very much, too.

Gary: Celine, you're American. Why do you live here in London?

Celine: Because I just love ___it___ here! The people are fantastic! I love them! And of course, my husband, Charles, is English, and I love him, too!

Gary: That's a very nice photo. Who are they?

Celine: My sons. That's Matt and that's Jack. They go to school here. My daughter's at school in the US. Her name's Lisa-Marie.

Gary: _____ does Lisa-Marie go to school in the US?

Celine: _____ she lives with her father. My first husband, you know—the actor Dan Brat. I hate _____ and all his movies. I never watch _____.

Gary: I see. So does Lisa-Marie visit you?

Celine: Oh, yes. She visits me every vacation. She's here with _____ now.

Gary: And is this a photo of _____ and Charles?

Celine: Oh, yes. It's us in Hawaii. It's our wedding. We're so happy together!

THAT

THIS

1 Look at the picture. Work with a partner. Ask and answer questions.

What's this?

It's a phone.

What's that?

It's a dog.

2 Ask and answer questions about things in your classroom.

What's that?

It's Marta's bag.

What's this?

It's a book.

What's that?

I don't know.

I like them!

3 Complete the sentences with an object pronoun.

1. Do you like ice cream?
   Yes, I love __it__ .
2. Do you like dogs?
   No, I hate _____ .
3. Do you like me?
   Of course I like _____!
4. Does your teacher teach you Spanish?
   No, she teaches _____ English.
5. Do you like your teacher?
   We like _____ very much.

T 7.3 Listen and check.

What do you like?

4 Ask and answer questions with a partner. Ask about …

soccer

vacations

your sister/brother

television

rock music

cats

chocolate

cell phones

computers

dogs

Do you like soccer?

Yes, I do. I love it.

No, I don't. I hate it.

It's all right.

Questions and answers

5 Work with a partner. Ask and answer the questions.

1. Why/Celine drink tea?   (… like …)
   Why does Celine drink tea?   _Because she likes it._
2. Why/you/eat oranges?   (… like …)
   _____   _____
3. Why/Annie want to marry Peter?   (… love …)
   _____   _____
4. Why/you eat Chinese food?   (… like …)
   _____   _____
5. Why/not like your math teacher?   (… gives … a lot of homework.)
   _____   _____
6. Why/Miguel buy presents for Maria? (… love …)
   _____   _____

T 7.4 Listen and check.

6 Match the questions and answers.

1. How do you come to school?	They start at nine o'clock.
2. What do you have for breakfast?	In an office in the center of town.
3. Who is your favorite pop group?	Three.
4. Where does your father work?	Not a lot. About two dollars.
5. Why do you want to learn English?	By bus.
6. How much money do you have?	Because it's an international language.
7. When do classes start at your school?	Toast and coffee.
8. How many languages does your teacher speak?	I don't have a favorite. I like a lot of groups.

T 7.5 Listen and check. Practice the questions.

Work with a partner. Ask and answer the questions about you.

Check it

7 Put a check (✓) next to the correct sentence.

1. ☐ What do you do on the weekend?
   ☐ Where do you do on the weekend?
2. ☐ Who is your boyfriend?
   ☐ When is your boyfriend?
3. ☐ How many money do you have?
   ☐ How much money do you have?
4. ☐ I don't drink tea. I don't like.
   ☐ I don't drink tea. I don't like it.
5. ☐ Our teacher gives us a lot of homework.
   ☐ Our teacher gives we a lot of homework.
6. ☐ She loves me and I love her.
   ☐ She loves my and I love she.

VOCABULARY

Adjectives

1 Match the words and pictures. Write sentences.

new	expensive	great	small	old	awful	hot	cold	cheap	big

7

3

1

It's great.

2

4

8

5

9

6

10

T 7.6 Listen and check. Practice the sentences.

2 Write the opposite adjectives. Choose a word from the box in Exercise 1.

Adjective	new	expensive	great	small	cold
Opposite					

READING AND WRITING
A postcard from San Francisco

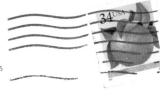

1 **T 7.7** Look at the postcard. Read and listen. Check the meaning of new words.

Dear Allen,

We're on vacation in San Francisco this week. Our hotel is very nice—old and comfortable. The people are very friendly.

The food is delicious (and cheap), and the cafes are wonderful!

San Francisco is beautiful. It's a big city, with a lot of new buildings, and it isn't expensive.

The weather is awful! It's wet and it's cold!

See you soon.

Love, **Diana** and **Davi**

(your Brazilian students!)

Allen Birch
The English School
120 Magazine Rd.
Boston, MA
02148

2 Answer the questions.
1. Who is the postcard from?
2. Where are they?
3. Why are they in San Francisco?
4. Is their vacation good?
5. What isn't good?

3 What adjectives do Diana and Davi use? Complete the chart.

	Adjectives
their hotel	nice, old, comfortable
people	
the food	
the cafes	
San Francisco	
the weather	

4 Write a postcard to a friend.

Dear ...
We're on vacation in ... and it's very ...
Our hotel is ...
The people are ...
The food is ... and it isn't ...
The weather ... hot, and ...
to the beach every day.
See you soon. *Love,*

EVERYDAY ENGLISH

Can I . . . ?

1 Write a number *1–5* (place) and a letter *a–e* (activity) for each picture.

PLACES	ACTIVITIES
1. a train station	a. try on a sweater
2. a cafe	b. change a traveler's check
3. a bank	c. have a tuna sandwich
4. an Internet cafe	d. buy a round-trip ticket
5. a clothing store	e. send an e-mail

2 [T 7.8] Listen to Keiko. She is in different places in town. Where is she in the conversations? What does she want? Choose from Exercise 1.

Where is she?	What does she want?
1. In a cafe.	To have a tuna sandwich.
2. _____	_____
3. _____	_____
4. _____	_____
5. _____	_____

3 Complete the conversations with a partner.

1. **A** Next, please!
   K Can I have __a__ __tuna__ __sandwich__, please?
   A OK.
   K How _____ is that?
   A _____ _____ ninety-five, please.
   K Here you are.
   A Thanks _____ _____.

2. **K** Hi. Can I _____ _____ this sweater, please?
   B _____ _____. The fitting rooms are over there.

3. **K** _____ _____ _____ _____ e-mail, please?
   C OK. Computer _____ _____.
   K _____ _____ is it?
   C Forty-five cents a minute. You pay at the end.

4. **D** Good morning. Can I help you?
   K Yes, please. _____ _____ _____ a traveler's check?
   D How much is it?
   K _____ dollars.
   D OK.

5. **K** _____ _____ _____ a round-trip ticket to Milford, please?
   E Sure.
   K How much _____ _____?
   E Eighteen _____, please.
   K Thank you.
   E Twenty dollars. Here's _____ _____, and $2.00 change.

[T 7.8] Listen and check.

Practice the conversations.

4 Work with a partner. Make more conversations with different information.

Student A
- a coffee
- this jacket
- a round-trip ticket to Dallas

Student B
- an ice cream
- this T-shirt
- a one-way ticket to Houston

8 Where I live

Rooms and furniture · *There is/are* · *any* · Prepositions · Directions

1 Do you live in a house or an apartment? Do you have a yard? Tell the class.

> *I live in an apartment.*

> *We don't have a yard.*

2 **T 8.1** Look at the picture. Listen and repeat the rooms of a house.

living room, dining room . . .

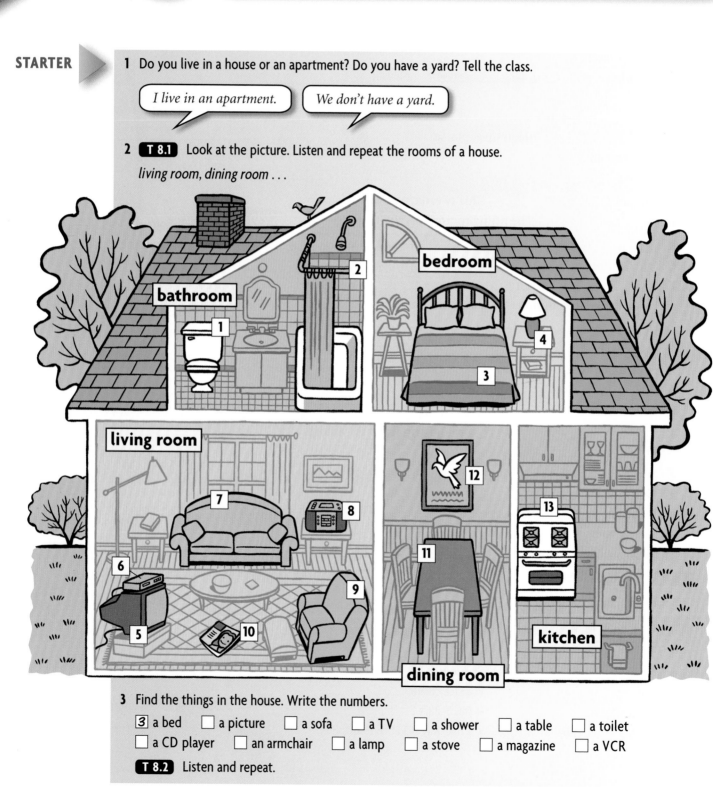

bathroom

bedroom

living room

dining room

kitchen

3 Find the things in the house. Write the numbers.

☑ 3 a bed ☐ a picture ☐ a sofa ☐ a TV ☐ a shower ☐ a table ☐ a toilet
☐ a CD player ☐ an armchair ☐ a lamp ☐ a stove ☐ a magazine ☐ a VCR

T 8.2 Listen and repeat.

JANET'S LIVING ROOM

There is / are, any

1 **T 8.3** Read and listen to Janet describing her living room. Complete the sentences.

My living room isn't very big, but I love it. There's a sofa, and there are two armchairs. __There__ 's a small table with a TV on it, and there _____ a lot of books. _____ a CD player, and _____ _____ some CDs. _____ _____ pictures on the wall, and _____ _____ two lamps. It's a very comfortable room.

2 Make sentences about Janet's living room.

- a sofa
- a lot of books
- a CD player
- a table
- two armchairs
- some CDs

> *There's a sofa.*

> *There are two armchairs.*

3 **T 8.4** Look at the questions and answers. Listen and repeat.

Is there a sofa?	Yes, there is.
Is there a computer?	No, there isn't.
Are there any armchairs?	Yes, there are.
Are there any photographs?	No, there aren't.

Practice the questions and answers with a partner.

GRAMMAR SPOT

Complete the sentences with *there is / there are*.

Affirmative	**There's** a sofa.	_____ two armchairs.
Question	_____ a TV?	**Are there** any photos?
Negative	**There isn't** a computer.	_____ any magazines.

▶▶ **Grammar Reference 8.1 and 8.2 p. 128**

---

4 Ask and answer questions about Janet's living room.

- a TV
- photographs
- a radio
- a CD player
- a telephone
- a VCR
- lamps
- pictures

> *Is there a TV?*

> *Yes, there is.*

> *Are there any photographs?*

> *No, there aren't.*

5 Work with a partner. Describe your living room.

> *In my living room there's a …*

> *There are a lot of …*

JANET'S BEDROOM
Prepositions

1 Look at the prepositions.

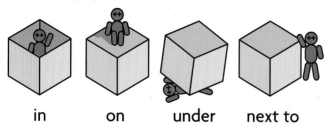

in   on   under   next to

2 Look at Janet's bedroom. Write a preposition from Exercise 1.

1. Janet's cell phone is _on_ the bed.
2. The magazine is _____ the phone.
3. Her CD player is _____ the floor _____ _____ the desk.
4. Her car keys are _____ the drawer.
5. Her bag is _____ the floor _____ the chair.
6. The books are _____ her bed.

T 8.5 Listen and check. Practice the sentences.

3 Ask and answer questions about Janet's things.

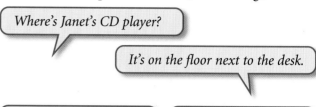

Where's Janet's CD player?

It's on the floor next to the desk.

Where are her car keys?   *They're in the drawer.*

Ask about her …

- CD player
- CDs
- lamp
- computer
- pens
- shoes
- car keys
- clothes
- credit cards

4 Close your eyes! Ask and answer questions about things in your classroom.

Where is Ali's dictionary?   *It's in his bag.*

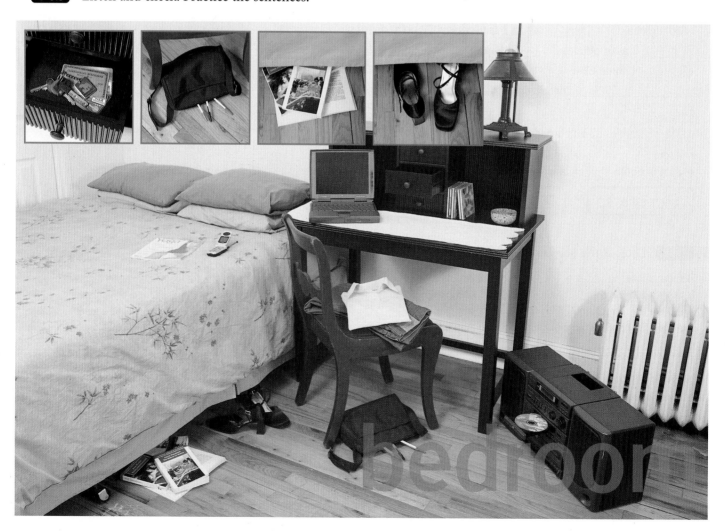

PRACTICE

Questions and answers

1 Put the words in the correct order to make a question.

1.

house   live   or   in   you   a

Do   apartment   an

<u>Do you live in a house or an apartment</u> ?

2.

bedrooms   How   many

there   How   are

_____ ?

3.

telephone   the   Is   in

there   kitchen   a

_____ ?

4.

living room   a   the

there   Is   in   television

_____ ?

5.

the   a   Is   under

VCR   television   there

_____ ?

6.

Are   in   your   books

bedroom   there

a lot of

_____ ?

7.

pictures   Are

wall   there   the   any

on

_____ ?

T 8.6 Listen and check.

2 Work with a partner. Ask and answer the questions about where you live.

Different rooms

3 Work with a partner.

Student A Look at the picture below.

Student B Look at the picture on p. 111.

Your pictures are different. Talk about your pictures to find six differences.

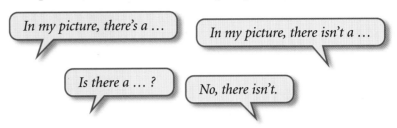

In my picture, there's a …

In my picture, there isn't a …

Is there a … ?

No, there isn't.

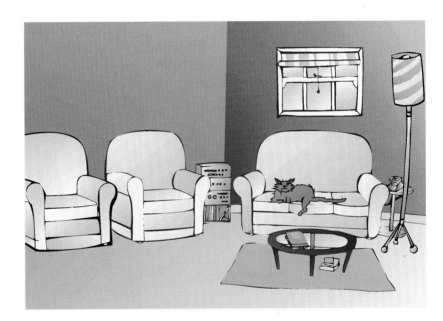

4 **T 8.7** Listen to a description of one of the rooms. Which room is it?

Check it

5 Put a check (✔) next to the correct sentence.

1. ☐ Is a sofa in the living room?
   ☐ Is there a sofa in the living room?
2. ☐ There's a CD player.
   ☐ There are a CD player.
3. ☐ Are there a lamps?
   ☐ Are there any lamps?
4. ☐ Your keys are in the drawer.
   ☐ Your keys are on the drawer.
5. ☐ The lamp is next to the bed.
   ☐ The lamp is next the bed.

Sydney

1 Look at the pictures of Sydney, Australia. Find these things in the pictures.

- the Opera House
- a beach
- a harbor
- a ferry
- windsurfing
- sailing
- a bridge
- a park

2 Read the text about Sydney on p. 57. Here are the five paragraph headings. Put them in the correct place.

What to do

What to eat

Where to stay

When to go

How to travel

T 8.8 Listen and check.

3 Complete the chart with an adjective or a noun from the text.

Adjective	Noun
old / new	buildings
	beaches
delicious	
	hotels in King's Cross
	hotels in the center
	stores
	Bondi Beach
fresh	
fast	
	buses

4 Answer the questions.

1. When are the best times to go?
2. Are all the hotels expensive?
3. What do people do … ?
   - on Pitt Street
   - at the harbor
   - at the beach
   - on Oxford Street
4. What restaurants are there in Sydney?
5. What is the best way to see Sydney?

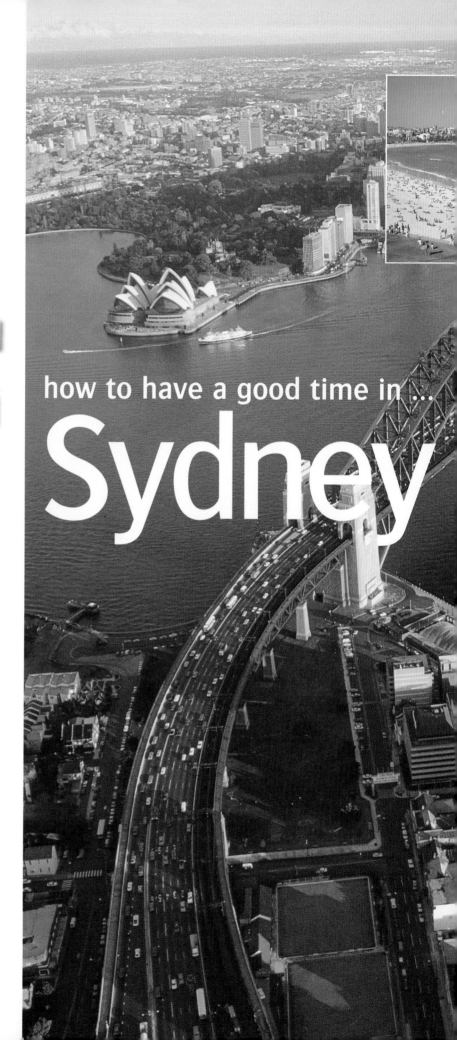

how to have a good time in …
Sydney

Sydney has everything you want in a city. It's beautiful, it has old and new buildings, there are fantastic beaches, and the food is delicious.

The best times to visit are the spring and fall. In the summer it is very hot.

There are cheap hotels in King's Cross. A room is about $50 a night. There are international hotels in the center. Here a room is about $150 a night.

Sydney has theaters and movie theaters, and of course, the Opera House. The best stores are on Pitt Street.

Go to the harbor. There are beaches, walks, parks, cafes, and, of course, the wonderful bridge.

Sydney has the famous Bondi Beach. People go swimming, surfing, windsurfing, and sailing.

For nightlife, there are a lot of clubs on Oxford Street.

There are restaurants from every country—Italian, Turkish, Lebanese, Japanese, Thai, Chinese, and Vietnamese. Australians eat a lot of seafood —it's very fresh!

There are fast trains and slow buses. The best way to see Sydney is by ferry.

LISTENING AND WRITING
My hometown

1 **T 8.9** Listen to Darren. He lives in Sydney. Put a check (✓) next to the things he talks about. Listen again. What does he say about them?

sailing	☐	_____
his brother	☑	He lives in a house with his brother.
surfing	☐	_____
train	☐	_____
movie theaters	☐	_____
the harbor	☐	_____
the Opera House	☐	_____
seafood	☐	_____
his girlfriend	☐	_____
Oxford Street	☐	_____
Japanese food	☐	_____
Manly Beach	☐	_____
ferry	☐	_____

2 In groups, talk about your hometown or a town you like.
- Where do you live?
- Where do you work/go to school?
- What do you do with your friends?
- Where do you go shopping?
- What do you do when you go out?

3 Write about a town you know. Use these paragraph headings and ideas.

What to do
There is a movie theater . . . The best stores . . . Go to . . .

What to eat
There are good restaurants on . . .

Where to stay
. . . is an expensive hotel. . . . is a cheap hotel.

When to visit
The best time to visit is . . .

How to travel
The best way to travel is . . .

EVERYDAY ENGLISH
Directions

1 Find the places on the map.

| bank | drugstore | movie theater | post office | newsstand | bookstore | supermarket | school | Internet cafe |

2 What do the signs mean?

| turn right | go straight ahead | turn left |

3 **T 8.10** Listen to the directions. Start from YOU ARE HERE on the map. Follow the directions. Where are you?

Go down Main Street. Turn right at the Grand Hotel onto Charles Street. It's next to the movie theater.

1. **At the drugstore.**
2. _____
3. _____
4. _____
5. _____

Look at the tapescript on p. 120. Practice the conversations.

4 Work with a partner. Have similar conversations.

Ask about …
- a movie theater
- a post office
- a newsstand
- a supermarket
- a theater
- a clothing store
- an Italian restaurant

Excuse me! Is there a … near here?

Yes. Go down …

5 Ask for and give directions in your town.

How do I get to the post office?

Go out of the school. Turn right …

Is it far?

About ten minutes.

9 Happy birthday!

Saying years · *was/were born* · Past Simple – irregular verbs · When's your birthday?

STARTER

1 **T 9.1** Listen and <u>underline</u> the years you hear. Say them.

1. <u>1426</u> / 1526   3. 1818 / 1880   5. 1951 / 1961
2. 1699 / 1799   4. 1939 / 1949   6. 2007 / 2010

2 What year is it now? What year was it last year?

❶	We say:	**1841**	eighteen forty-one
		1916	nineteen sixteen
	but	**2000**	two thousand
		2008	two thousand eight
		2015	two thousand fifteen

T 9.2 Listen and repeat.

WHEN WERE THEY BORN?

was/were born

1 **T 9.3** Do you know these people? When were they born?
Listen and write the years.

Leonardo da Vinci | painter and scientist
born _____ Tuscany, Italy.

Marie Curie | scientist
born _____ Warsaw, Poland.

2 **T 9.4** Listen and repeat.

He was a painter.
He was born in 1452.

She was a scientist.
She was born in 1867.

I was born in 1979.

3 Ask and answer questions with other students.

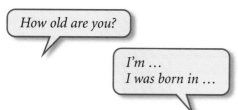

How old are you?

I'm ...
I was born in ...

4 **T 9.5** Listen to the questions and answers. Practice them.

When were you born?	I was born in 1986.
When was he born?	He was born in 1975.
When was she born?	She was born in 1991.
When were they born?	They were born in 2001.

GRAMMAR SPOT

Complete the chart of the verb *to be*.

	Present	Past
I	am	was
You	are	
He/She/It	is	
We	are	were
They	are	

▶▶ **Grammar Reference 9.1 p. 128**

---

5 **T 9.6** This is Calico Jones. Listen to her talking about her family. Write when they were born.

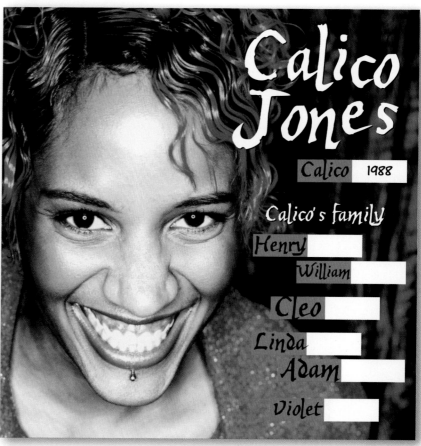

Calico Jones

| Calico | 1988 |

Calico's family
Henry
William
Cleo
Linda
Adam
Violet

Ask and answer questions about the people.

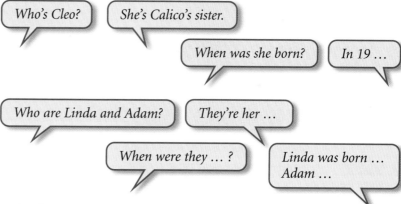

Who's Cleo?

She's Calico's sister.

When was she born?

In 19 ...

Who are Linda and Adam?

They're her ...

When were they ... ?

Linda was born ...
Adam ...

6 Write the names of some people in your family. Ask and answer questions about them.

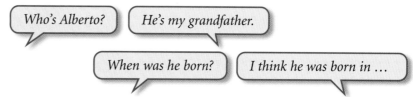

Who's Alberto?

He's my grandfather.

When was he born?

I think he was born in ...

7 Tell the class about your partner's family.

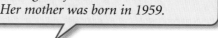

Ana's grandfather was born in 1936.
Her mother was born in 1959.

PRACTICE

Who were they?

1 Do you know the people in the photographs?
Match the people 1–8 and jobs.

5 singer	☐ musician	☐ actor
☐ writer	☐ painter	☐ princess
☐ politician	☐ race-car driver	

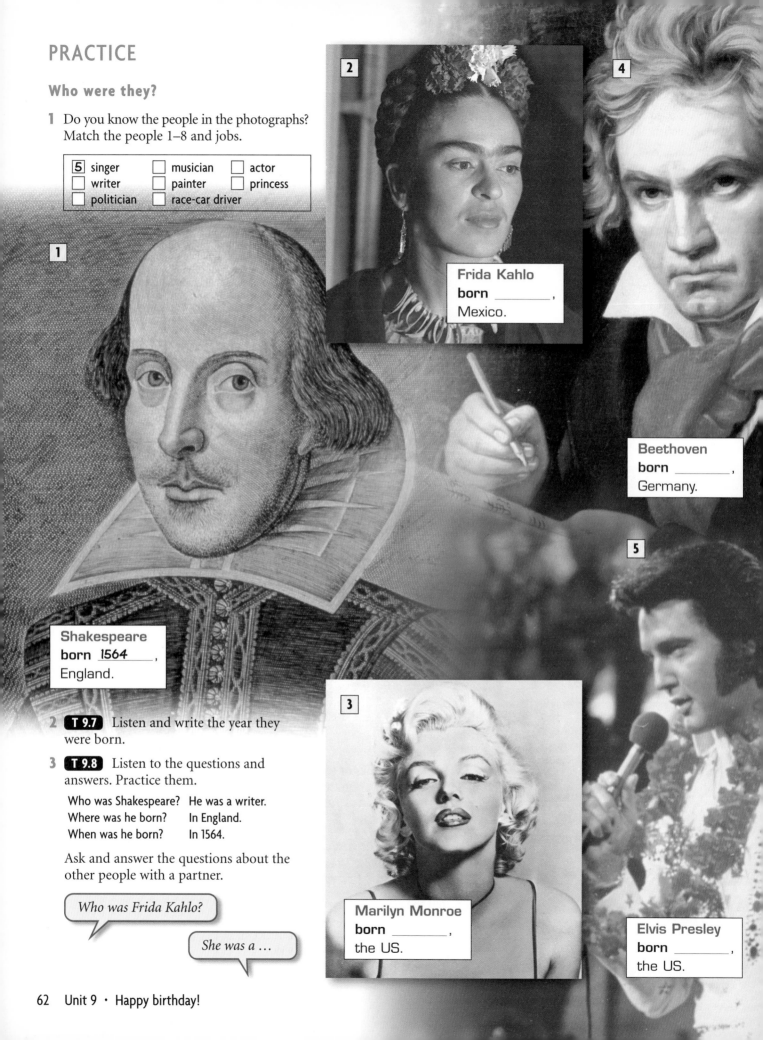

Frida Kahlo
born _____,
Mexico.

Beethoven
born _____,
Germany.

Shakespeare
born 1564 _____,
England.

2 **T 9.7** Listen and write the year they
were born.

3 **T 9.8** Listen to the questions and
answers. Practice them.

Who was Shakespeare?   He was a writer.
Where was he born?   In England.
When was he born?   In 1564.

Ask and answer the questions about the
other people with a partner.

Who was Frida Kahlo?

She was a ...

Marilyn Monroe
born _____,
the US.

Elvis Presley
born _____,
the US.

**Diana Spencer
born _____ ,
England.**

**Ayrton Senna
born _____ ,
Brazil.**

**Indira Ghandi
born _____ ,
India.**

Negatives and pronunciation

4 **T 9.9** Listen and repeat.

Shakespeare was a painter.

No, he wasn't. He was a writer.

Shakespeare and Diana were Brazilian.

No, they weren't. They were English.

> ❗ /wəz/
> **1** He was a painter.
> /wʌznt/
> No, he wasn't.
> *wasn't* = was not
> /wər/
> **2** They were American.
> /wərnt/
> No, they weren't.
> *weren't* = were not

5 Write the correct information.

1. Ayrton Senna was an actor.
   No, he _____ .
2. Marie Curie was a princess.
   No, she _____ .
3. Marilyn Monroe and Elvis Presley were Mexican.
   No, they _____ .
4. Beethoven was a scientist.
   No, he _____ .
5. Leonardo da Vinci and Frida Kahlo were musicians.
   No, they _____ .
6. Indira Ghandi was a singer.
   No, she _____ .

T 9.10 Listen, check, and repeat. Practice the sentences.

Today and yesterday

6 What is true for you? Tell a partner.

Today is . . . Yesterday was . . .	Monday, Tuesday, Wednesday . . .
I'm . . . I was . . .	at school / at home / at work . . .
The weather is . . . The weather was . . .	hot / cold / wet / beautiful / awful . . .
My parents are . . . My parents were . . .	at work / at home . . .

Check it

7 Complete the sentences with *was, wasn't, were,* or *weren't.*

1. Where _____ your mother born?
2. When _____ your parents born?
3. No, my parents _____ both born in 1951. My *father* _____ born in 1951, and my *mother* in 1953.
4. Yes, I _____ in New York in 1999.
5. _____ he at home yesterday? No, he _____ .
6. _____ you at work yesterday? Yes, we _____ .
7. _____ they at school yesterday morning? No, they _____ .

VOCABULARY AND READING

Past Simple—irregular verbs

1 Match the present and the past forms.
Look at the irregular verb list on p. 137.

Present	Past
are	was
is	were
buy	went
go	said
say	bought
see	took
take	saw

T 9.11 Listen, check, and repeat.

▶▶ **Grammar Reference 9.2 p. 128**

2 Look at the pictures. They tell a story.
Match the sentences and pictures.

a. **They bought the painting for 1,400 francs.**

b. **The man in the market was very upset.**

c. **They took the painting to an expert in Paris.**

d. **Three friends went shopping at a market in France.**

e. **The expert said the painting was worth 500 million francs.**

f. **They saw a dirty, old painting for sale.**

3 Read the story. Complete it with an irregular verb from Exercise 1.

"We're millionaires!"

Florence Bayes in Paris

In August 1999 three friends, Charles Proust, Robert Fadat, and Georges Leclerc, _**were**_ on vacation in the town of Laraque in France. On Sunday they _____ shopping at the market and they _____ a dirty, old painting. They _____ it for 1,400 francs and they _____ it to Paris. In Paris, an expert said that the painting was by Leonardo da Vinci and it _____ worth 500,000,000 francs. The man at the Laraque market said, "I was happy to sell the painting, but now I'm very upset. I don't want to think about it!"

T 9.12 Listen and check.

Read the story to a partner.

4 Look at the pictures only and tell the story to a partner.

When's your birthday?

สุขสันต์วันเกิด

Bon Anniversaire

1 These are the months of the year. What is the correct order?

March   June   October   April   February

November   May   July   September   August

January
1 2 3 4 5 6 7 8 9 10 11 12 13 14 15 16 17 18 19 20 21 22 23 24 25 26 27 28 29 30 31

1 2 3 4 5 6 7 8 9 10 11 12 13 14 15 16 17 18 19 20 21 22 23 24 25 26 27 28

1 2 3 4 5 6 7 8 9 10 11 12 13 14 15 16 17 18 19 20 21 22 23 24 25 26 27 28 29 30 31

1 2 3 4 5 6 7 8 9 10 11 12 13 14 15 16 17 18 19 20 21 22 23 24 25 26 27 28 29 30

1 2 3 4 5 6 7 8 9 10 11 12 13 14 15 16 17 18 19 20 21 22 23 24 25 26 27 28 29 30 31

1 2 3 4 5 6 7 8 9 10 11 12 13 14 15 16 17 18 19 20 21 22 23 24 25 26 27 28 29 30

1 2 3 4 5 6 7 8 9 10 11 12 13 14 15 16 17 18 19 20 21 22 23 24 25 26 27 28 29 30 31

1 2 3 4 5 6 7 8 9 10 11 12 13 14 15 16 17 18 19 20 21 22 23 24 25 26 27 28 29 30

1 2 3 4 5 6 7 8 9 10 11 12 13 14 15 16 17 18 19 20 21 22 23 24 25 26 27 28 29 30

1 2 3 4 5 6 7 8 9 10 11 12 13 14 15 16 17 18 19 20 21 22 23 24 25 26 27 28 29 30 31

1 2 3 4 5 6 7 8 9 10 11 12 13 14 15 16 17 18 19 20 21 22 23 24 25 26 27 28 29 30

December
1 2 3 4 5 6 7 8 9 10 11 12 13 14 15 16 17 18 19 20 21 22 23 24 25 26 27 28 29 30 31

T 9.13 Listen and check. Say the months around the class.

2 Which month is your birthday? Tell the class.

> My birthday's in September.

> So is **my** birthday!

How many birthdays are in each month? Which month has the most?

3 **T 9.14** Listen and repeat the numbers.

first **(1st)**   second **(2nd)**   third **(3rd)**

fourth **(4th)**   fifth **(5th)**

sixth **(6th)**   seventh **(7th)**

eighth **(8th)**   ninth **(9th)**

tenth **(10th)**   eleventh **(11th)**

twelfth **(12th)**   thirteenth **(13th)**

fourteenth **(14th)**   fifteenth **(15th)**

4 Say these numbers.

16th	17th	18th	19th	20th	21st	22nd	23rd
24th	25th	26th	27th	28th	29th	30th	31st

T 9.15 Listen and check.

5 **T 9.16** Listen and write the numbers. Practice them.

January __first__

March _____

April _____

May _____

June _____

August _____

November _____

December _____

!	1	We say:	*January third*
			March tenth
	2	We write:	*January 3*
			January 3, 2003
			1/3/03

6 When is your birthday? Do you know the time you were born? Ask and answer in groups.

> *When's your birthday?*

> *It's on March third.*

> *What time were you born?*

> *At two o'clock in the morning.*

Tell the class.

> *I was born on July 20, 1978, at two o'clock in the morning.*

10 We had a good time!

STARTER

1 What day is it today? What day was it yesterday?
What's the date today? What date was it yesterday?

2 Match a line in **A** with a time expression in **B**.
T 10.1 Listen, check, and repeat.

A	B
1. We're at school	now.
2. You were at home	yesterday.
3. I went to Australia	in 1997.
4. She lives in Chicago	
5. They bought their house	
6. It was cold and wet	

YESTERDAY

Past Simple – regular and irregular

1 **T 10.2** Read the sentences and listen to
Becky. Put a check (✓) next to the things
she did yesterday.

2 Tell the class what she did.

> *Yesterday she got up late and
> she had a big .... Then she ...*

Yesterday she . . .

- ✓ got up late
- ☐ had a big breakfast
- ☐ played tennis
- ☐ went to work / school
- ☐ went shopping
- ☐ stayed home
- ☐ bought a newspaper
- ☐ listened to music
- ☐ saw some friends
- ☐ watched TV
- ☐ worked on a computer
- ☐ cooked dinner
- ☐ went to bed early

GRAMMAR SPOT

1 Write the Past Simple of these regular verbs.

/t/	work	watch	cook
	worked	_____	_____

/d/	play	stay	listen
	played	_____	_____

What are the last two letters?

T 10.3 Listen and repeat.

2 Write the Past Simple of these regular verbs.

/ɪd/	visit	want	hate
	_____	_____	_____

T 10.4 Listen and repeat.

3 The Past Simple is the same in all persons.
I/You/He/She/It/We/They worked.

▶▶ Grammar Reference 10.1 p. 128

---

3 Underline the things in the list that you did yesterday. Talk to a partner.

> *Yesterday I got up early and went ...*

Questions and negatives

4 [T 10.5] It's Monday morning. Listen to Becky and Dan. Complete their conversation.

B Hi, Dan. Did you have a good weekend?

D Yes, I did, thanks.

B What did you do yesterday?

D Well, yesterday morning I got up early and I __played__ tennis with some friends.

B You _____ _____ early on Sunday!

D I know, I know. I don't usually get up early on Sunday.

B Did you go out yesterday afternoon?

D No, I didn't. I just _____ home and _____ basketball on TV.

B Ugh, basketball! What did you do yesterday evening?

D Oh, I didn't do much. I _____ a little on my computer. I didn't go to bed late, about 11:00.

5 Complete the questions and answers from the conversation.

1. **B** __Did__ you __have__ a good weekend?
   D Yes, I did.
2. **B** What _____ you _____ yesterday?
   D I played tennis.
3. **B** _____ you _____ out yesterday afternoon?
   D No, I didn't.
4. **B** What _____ you _____ yesterday evening?
   D I didn't do much. I _____ go to bed late.

[T 10.6] Listen and check. Practice the questions and answers with a partner.

> ### GRAMMAR SPOT
>
> **Past Simple questions and negatives**
> **1** We make the question and negative with *did* and *didn't* in all persons.
>
> | | |
> |---|---|
> | **Did** you **get up** early? | Yes, I **did**. |
> | **Did** she **get up** early? | No, she **didn't**. |
> | We **didn't go** to work. | *didn't* = did not |
> | They **didn't go** to work. | |
>
> [T 10.7] Listen and repeat the sentences.
>
> **2** We use *do / does* in the Present Simple and *did* in the Past Simple.
>
> What **do** you **do** every morning?
> What **did** you **do** yesterday morning?
> She **doesn't** play tennis every Sunday.
> She **didn't** play tennis last Sunday.
>
> ▶▶ **Grammar Reference 10.2 p. 128**

6 Look at the list in Exercise 1 on p. 68. Ask and answer questions about Dan's weekend.

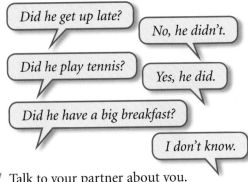

Did he get up late?
No, he didn't.
Did he play tennis?
Yes, he did.
Did he have a big breakfast?
I don't know.

7 Talk to your partner about you. What *didn't* you do last weekend?

I didn't get up early.
I didn't play tennis.

PRACTICE

Did you have a good weekend?

1 Put a check (✓) next to the things you did last weekend.

LAST WEEKEND			
Did you . . . ?	**You**	**Teacher**	**Partner**
go to the movies	☐	☐	☐
go shopping	☐	☐	☐
eat in a restaurant	☐	☐	☐
see your friends	☐	☐	☐
play soccer	☐	☐	☐
go to a party	☐	☐	☐
do a lot of homework	☐	☐	☐
do a lot of housework	☐	☐	☐

2 Ask your teacher the questions. Put a check (✓) next to the things she/he did last weekend.

> *Did you go to the movies?*

> *Yes, I did./No, I didn't.*

3 Ask a partner the questions. Put a check (✓) next to the things she/he did last weekend.

Tell the class about you and your partner.

> *Maria went to the movies, but I didn't. I went shopping.*

4 Work with a partner.

- **Student A** Go to page 112.
- **Student B** Go to page 114.

5 Make more questions with *did*.

1. What/see? — <u>What did you see?</u>
2. What/buy? _____
3. What/have? _____
4. Who/see? _____
5. Where/play? _____
6. What time/leave? _____
7. How much homework/do? _____
8. How much housework/do? _____

T 10.8 Listen and check. What does the man say before the questions?

6 **T 10.9** Listen to the conversations. Practice them with your partner.

A Did you go to the movies last weekend?
B Yes, I did.
A What did you see?
B I saw *The Boy from Bangkok.*
A Was it good?
B Yes, it was.

A Did you eat in a restaurant?
B Yes, we did.
A What did you have?
B We had steak and fries.
A Was it good?
B No, it wasn't. It was awful!

Make similar conversations with your partner. Use the activities in Exercise 1 and the questions in Exercise 4.

7 Complete the short answers with *do/don't*, *does/doesn't*, or *did/didn't*.

1. Do you work in New York? — No, I <u>don't</u>.
2. Did she like the movie? — Yes, she <u>did</u>.
3. Does he watch TV every night? — Yes, he _____.
4. Did you go out last night? — No, we _____.
5. Did he go to the party? — Yes, he _____.
6. Do you buy a newspaper every morning? — Yes, I _____.
7. Does she usually go to bed late? — No, she _____.
8. Did they have a good time? — No, they _____.

T 10.10 Listen and check. Practice the questions and answers with a partner.

Check it

8 Put a check (✓) next to the correct sentence.

1. ☐ She bought an expensive car.
   ☐ She buyed an expensive car.
2. ☐ Did they went shopping yesterday?
   ☐ Did they go shopping yesterday?
3. ☐ What did you go last weekend?
   ☐ Where did you go last weekend?
4. ☐ We didn't see our friends.
   ☐ We no saw our friends.
5. ☐ "Did you like the movie?" "Yes, I liked."
   ☐ "Did you like the movie?" "Yes, I did."
6. ☐ I played tennis yesterday.
   ☐ I play tennis yesterday.

VOCABULARY AND SPEAKING
Sports and leisure

1 Match a picture and an activity.

windsurfing

baseball

ice skating

cards

tennis

skiing   soccer

golf

sailing

walking

swimming

ice hockey

dancing

2 Write the activities in the correct column.

play	go + -ing
play tennis	go skiing

3 Ask and answer questions about the activities with a partner.

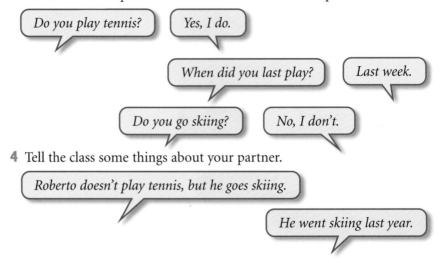

Do you play tennis?

Yes, I do.

When did you last play?

Last week.

Do you go skiing?

No, I don't.

4 Tell the class some things about your partner.

Roberto doesn't play tennis, but he goes skiing.

He went skiing last year.

LISTENING AND SPEAKING
Vacations

1 Say the months of the year. What are the four seasons?
When do you usually go on vacation?

> *We usually go on vacation in …*

2 **T 10.11** Listen to Bill and Kelly talking about vacations.
<u>Underline</u> what they say.

A

They usually …
go in the <u>summer</u> / spring.
go to *Florida* / *California*.
stay in a *hotel* / *house*.
eat in *the hotel* / *restaurants*.
go *swimming* / *sailing*.
play *tennis* / *golf*.
have / *don't have* a good time.

B

Last year they …
went in the *fall* / <u>winter.</u>
went to *Colorado* / *Vermont*.
stayed in a *hotel* / *an apartment*.
cooked their own meals / *ate in restaurants*.
went *skiing* / *ice skating* / *walking*.
played *cards* / *ice hockey*.
had / *didn't have* a good time.

3 Ask and answer questions with a partner
about Bill and Kelly's vacation.
- When / go?
- Where / go?
- Where / stay?
- Where / eat?
- What / do?
- … have a good time?

> *When do they usually go on vacation?*

> *In the summer.*

> *When did they go last year?*

> *They went in the winter.*

WRITING
My last vacation

1 Complete the sentences about Bill and Kelly's last vacation. Use a negative, then an affirmative in the Past Simple.

1. Last year Bill and Kelly __didn't go__ on vacation in the summer.
   They __went__ in the winter.
2. They _____ _____ to California.
   They _____ to Colorado.
3. They _____ _____ in a hotel.
   They _____ in an apartment.
4. They _____ _____ in restaurants.
   They _____ their own meals.
5. They _____ _____ swimming.
   They _____ skiing.

T 10.12 Listen and check.

2 Write about your last vacation.

My Last Vacation
Last ...
I went on vacation with ...
We went to ...
We stayed in ...
Every day we ...
We (sometimes/usually) ...
The weather was ...
We had/didn't have ...

Read it to the class.

Filling in forms

1 Jennifer Cotter wants to join a sports center. Look at her application form.

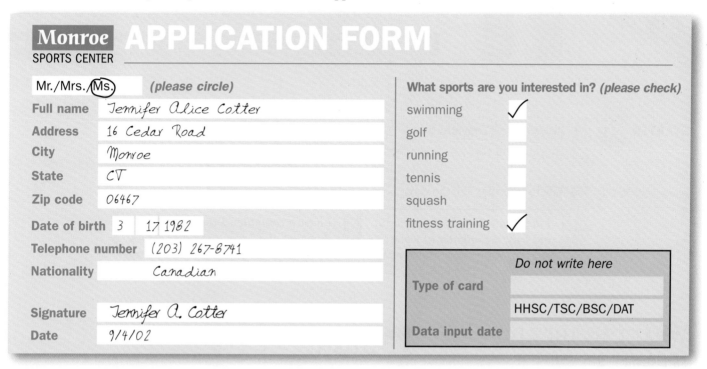

Monroe SPORTS CENTER **APPLICATION FORM**

Mr./Mrs./(Ms.) *(please circle)*

Full name	Jennifer Alice Cotter
Address	16 Cedar Road
City	Monroe
State	CT
Zip code	06467
Date of birth	3 17 1982
Telephone number	(203) 267-8741
Nationality	Canadian
Signature	Jennifer A. Cotter
Date	9/4/02

What sports are you interested in? *(please check)*

swimming	✓
golf	
running	
tennis	
squash	
fitness training	✓

Do not write here

Type of card

HHSC/TSC/BSC/DAT

Data input date

2 Fill in the same form for you.

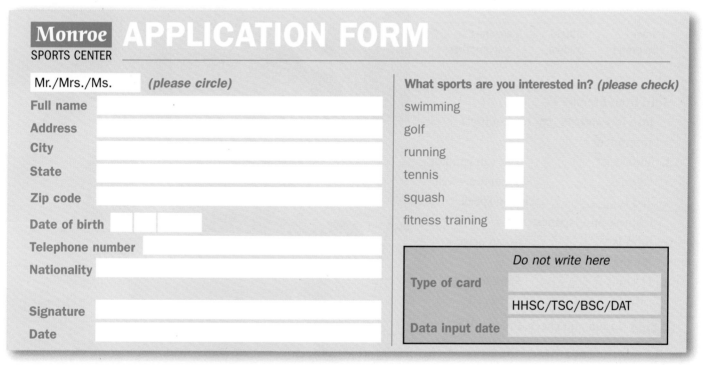

Monroe SPORTS CENTER **APPLICATION FORM**

Mr./Mrs./Ms. *(please circle)*

Full name	
Address	
City	
State	
Zip code	
Date of birth	
Telephone number	
Nationality	
Signature	
Date	

What sports are you interested in? *(please check)*

swimming	
golf	
running	
tennis	
squash	
fitness training	

Do not write here

Type of card

HHSC/TSC/BSC/DAT

Data input date

3 Work in groups. Look at your application forms. Who is interested in what?

Gabriel and I are both interested in golf.

Maria is interested in fitness training, but I'm not.

11

We can do it!

can/can't · Requests and offers · Verbs and nouns that go together · What's the problem?

STARTER

1 Do you have a computer?

Do you use it for . . .
- homework?
- e-mail?
- shopping?
- computer games?
- the Internet?

2 Talk to a partner. Tell the class.

> *I don't have a computer at home, but I use a computer at work.*

> *I have a computer. I use it for shopping and I play computer games.*

WHAT CAN THEY DO?
can/can't

1 Match the words and photos.

farmer	athlete	architect
interpreter	student	grandmother

2 Complete the sentences with *a* or *an* and a word from Exercise 1.

1. Josh is __a student__. He can use a computer.
2. Tamika is _____. She can run fast.
3. Laura is _____. She can draw well.
4. Ted is _____. He can speak Chinese and Japanese.
5. John is _____. He can drive a tractor.
6. Helen is _____. She can make cakes.

T 11.1 Listen and check. Practice the sentences.

3 Tell a partner what you can do from the list in Exercise 2.

> *I can use a computer and I can make cakes.*

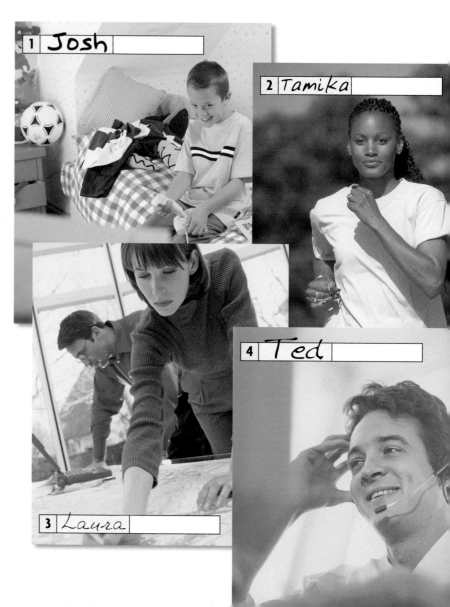

1 Josh

2 Tamika

3 Laura

4 Ted

Questions and negatives

4 **T 11.2** Listen and repeat the questions and answers.

Can Josh use a computer? Yes, he can.
Can you use a computer? Yes, I can.
Can Laura draw well? Yes, she can.
Can you draw well? No, I can't. I can't draw at all!

5 Ask and answer more questions with a partner. First ask about the people, then ask about your partner.

> *Can Tamika run fast?*

> *Yes, she can.*

> *Can you run fast?*

> *No, I can't.*

GRAMMAR SPOT

1 *Can/can't* have the same form for all persons.

I/You/He/She/It/We/They	can	draw.
	can't	*(can't = can not = negative)*

2 There is no *do/does* in the question.
I **can** speak Korean. **Can** you speak Korean?

3 **T 11.3** Listen and repeat the different pronunciations of *can*.
He can /kən/ speak Spanish. They can't /kænt/ speak Spanish.
Can /kən/ you speak Spanish? Yes, I can /kæn/.

▶▶ **Grammar Reference 11.1 p. 129**

5 John

6 Helen

6 **T 11.4** Read and listen to Josh and Teresa. Complete the conversation.

T Can you use a computer, Josh?
J Yes, of course I __can__. All my friends _____. I use a computer at school and at _____.
T That's very good. What other things can you do?
J Well, I can _____ fast—very fast—and I can draw a little. I can draw planes and _____ really well but I can't drive a car, of course. When I grow up I want to be a farmer and _____ a tractor.
T And I know you can speak French.
J Yes, I can. I _____ speak French very well because my dad's Canadian, from Quebec. We sometimes _____ French at home.
T Can you speak any other languages?
J No, I _____. I can't speak Spanish or Portuguese, just French—and English of course! And I can cook! I can _____ cakes. My grandmother makes delicious cakes and I sometimes help her. Yesterday we made a big chocolate cake!

Practice the conversation with a partner.

7 Answer the questions about Josh.
1. What can Josh do?
2. What can't Josh do?
3. Does he use a computer at school?
4. What does he want to be when he grows up?
5. Why can he speak French well?
6. What did he do yesterday?

PRACTICE

Pronunciation

1 **T 11.5** Listen and <u>underline</u> what you hear, *can* or *can't*.

1. I <u>can</u> / *can't* use a computer.
2. She *can* / *can't* speak Thai.
3. He *can* / *can't* speak English very well.
4. Why *can* / *can't* you come to my party?
5. We *can* / *can't* understand our teacher.
6. They *can* / *can't* read music.
7. *Can* / *Can't* we have an ice cream?
8. *Can* / *Can't* cats swim?

T 11.5 Listen again and repeat.

Can you or can't you?

2 **T 11.6** Listen to Tito. Put a check (✓) next to the things he can do.

Can . . . ?	Tito	You	T	S
speak Spanish	✓	☐	☐	☐
speak Japanese	☐	☐	☐	☐
speak English very well	☐	☐	☐	☐
drive a car	☐	☐	☐	☐
ride a horse	☐	☐	☐	☐
ski	☐	☐	☐	☐
cook	☐	☐	☐	☐
play the piano	☐	☐	☐	☐
play the guitar	☐	☐	☐	☐

T 11.6 Listen again and check.

3 Complete the chart about you. Then ask and answer the questions with the teacher and another student.

> *Can you speak Japanese?*

> *No, I can't. Can you?*

> *I can understand it but I can't speak it.*

4 Compare yourself with the teacher and other students.

> *Isabel and I can speak Spanish. She can speak French too, but I can't.*

Tito

Requests and offers

5 Use the words to write questions with *Can*.

me **tell** time you **the** please

1. Can you tell me the time, please ?

come to my **you** party

2. Can _____ ?

speak you more slowly **please**

3. Can _____ ?

help I you

4. Can _____ ?

have a cold I **drink** please

5. Can _____ ?

6 Match questions in Exercise 5 with these answers.

a. Yes, of course. Do you want soda or orange juice?
b. Yes, please. I want to buy this postcard.
c. It's about three thirty.
d. I'm sorry. Can you understand now?
e. I'm sorry. I can't. It's my grandmother's birthday.

T 11.7 Listen and check. Practice the requests with a partner. Continue the conversations.

> *Can you tell me the time, please?*

> *It's about three thirty.*

> *Thank you.*

> *You're welcome.*

Check it

7 Put a check (✓) next to the correct sentence.

1. ☐ I no can understand.
   ☐ I can't understand.

2. ☐ He can speak three languages.
   ☐ He cans speak three languages.

3. ☐ What you can see?
   ☐ What can you see?

4. ☐ Can you swim fast?
   ☐ Do you can swim fast?

5. ☐ "Can they come to the party?"
      "They no can."
   ☐ "Can they come to the party?"
      "No, they can't."

6. ☐ Does she can play tennis?
   ☐ Can she play tennis?

The things you can do on the Internet!

1 Match the verbs and nouns.

Verbs	Nouns
listen to	a reservation
watch	a CD
play	a magazine
read	a video
chat with	a friend
make	chess

2 Where do you find these addresses? What does *www* mean?

www.shopping.co.au

www.bbc.co.uk

www.chatshop.com

www.weatherpage.vancouver.bc.ca

3 What do you know about the Internet? Discuss these questions.

- When did the Internet start?
- Why did it start?
- What can you do on the Internet?

> *You can get a weather forecast.*

4 **T 11.8** Read and listen to the text about the Internet. Answer the questions in Exercise 3.

5 Are the sentences true (✔) or false (✗). Correct the false (✗) sentences.

1. The Internet started in the 1980s.
2. Telephone companies started it.
3. It started in the United States.
4. There is an international computer language.

6 The list is endless!

Work in groups. Do you know any good web sites? Tell the class.

Its history

The Internet started in the 1960s. The United States Department of Defense started it because they wanted a computer network to help the American military. In the 1970s, scientists worked on it. Then in the 1980s, telephone companies made it possible to communicate on the computer network in many more countries. An international computer language was born, and the Net went worldwide.

What can it do?

You can use the Internet for many things. You can shop for a car or a house; you can plan a vacation; you can watch a video; you can read an Australian newspaper or a Japanese magazine; you can buy books and CDs from North and South America; you can play chess with a partner in Moscow; or you can just chat with people from all over the world. The list is endless!

7 **T 11.9** Listen to the people. When and why do they use the Internet? Complete the chart.

	When?	Why?
Carmen	every day	help with homework
Anela		
Tito		
Liam		
Tommy		
April		

T 11.9 Listen again and check.

Getting Information

8 Work with a partner.

Student A Go to page 112.
Student B Go to page 114.

EVERYDAY ENGLISH

What's the problem?

1 Here are some problems. Check that you understand them.

"I don't understand this word."

"The TV's broken."

"This ticket machine doesn't work."

"I'm lost."

2 Complete the conversations with the problems from Exercise 1.

1. **A** Come on! It's time to go to the airport.
   B But ___I can't find my passport___ .
   A You put it in your bag.
   B Did I? Oh, yes. Here it is! *Phew!*

2. **A** Excuse me!
   B Yes?
   A _____.
   I put in two dollars, but I didn't get a ticket.
   B Did you push this button?
   A Oh! No, I didn't.
   B Ah, well. There you are.
   A Thank you very much.

3. **A** Excuse me!
   B Yes?
   A Can you help me?
   _____.
   B Where do you want to go?
   A To the Sherwood Hotel.
   B Go straight ahead. About 200 meters. It's on your left.
   A Thank you.

T 11.10 Listen and check.

3 Practice the conversations with a partner. Learn two conversations and act them for the class.

"I can't find my passport."

"I forgot your birthday."

4. **A** _____.
   B Check it in your dictionary.
   A My dictionary's at home. Can I borrow yours?
   B OK. No problem. Here you are.

5. **A** Oh, no!
   B What's the matter?
   A _____.
   B Good! Maybe we can talk this evening.
   A But I want to watch a movie.
   B Then go to the movie theater.

6. **A** I'm really sorry.
   _____.
   B It doesn't matter.
   A It was on the tenth, wasn't it?
   B Yes, it was.
   A Well, here are some flowers.
   B Oh, thank you. They're beautiful.

12 Thank you!

want and *would like* · Food and drink · In a restaurant · Going shopping

1 Match the activities and the places.

A	B
buy stamps	in a bank
buy a dictionary	in a music store
buy a computer magazine	in a bookstore
change money	in an Internet cafe
buy a CD	in a cafe
get a cup of coffee	in a post office
send an e-mail	at a newsstand

2 Make sentences beginning with *You can . . .*   *You can buy stamps in a post office.*

T 12.1 Listen and check.

A TRIP INTO TOWN
want and *would like*

1 Look at Enrique's "to do" list.
What does he want?

He wants a stamp.

He wants to change his money.

TO DO

a stamp for a
letter to Venezuela

change my money

Gary Alright's new CD

send an e-mail to
Rosa in England

a Spanish/English
dictionary

a "PC Worldwide"
computer magazine

2 **T 12.2** Read and listen to Enrique's conversations in town. Complete the sentences.

1. **E** Good morning. _I'd like_____
   a stamp for this letter to
   Venezuela, please.
   A That's 80¢.
   E Here you are.
   A Here's your stamp, and 20¢
   change.
   E Thanks a lot. Bye.

2. **E** _____ a cup of
   coffee, please.
   B _Would you like_____ milk and
   sugar?
   E No. Black, please.
   B All right. Here you are. A
   dollar fifty, please.

3. **E** Hi. _____ to buy
   a Spanish / English dictionary.
   C OK. _____ a big
   dictionary or a minidictionary?
   E Just a minidictionary, please.
   C This one is $6.50.
   E That's good. Thank you very
   much.

3 **T 12.3** Listen and repeat.

> I'd like a stamp.

> I'd like a cup of coffee.

> Would you like milk and sugar?

> I'd like to buy a dictionary.

> Would you like a big dictionary
> or a minidictionary?

Work with a partner. Practice the conversations in Exercise 2.

GRAMMAR SPOT

1 *I'd like . . .* (*'d* = would) is more polite than *I want . . . .*
   I'd like a cup of coffee, please.
   I'd like to buy a dictionary, please.

2 We offer things using *Would you like . . . ?*
   Would you like a cup of tea? No, thank you.
   Would you like to come to a party on Saturday? Yes, please.

▶▶ **Grammar Reference 12.1 p. 129**

---

4 **T 12.4** Listen to more conversations with
Enrique. Where is he? Write a number *1–5*.

☐ a newsstand
☐ an Internet cafe
☐ a music store
☐ a bank
☐ a movie theater

Look at the tapescript on p. 122. Practice
the conversations.

PRACTICE

What would you like?

1 Your friend is at your house. Make him/her feel at home!
Use the ideas.

- a drink
- a cup of coffee
- a sandwich
- some cake
- listen to music
- play cards
- watch a video
- play a computer game

> *Would you like a drink?*

> *Yes, please./No, thanks.*

> *What would you like?*

> *Orange juice, please.*

> *Would you like to listen to music?*

> *That's a good idea!*

It's my birthday!

2 **T 12.5** Listen to these people. It's their birthday soon.
Complete the chart.

	What would she/he like?	What would she/he like to do in the evening?
Suzanne		
Tom		
Alice		

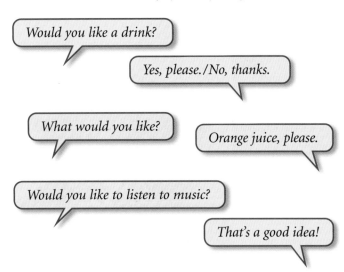

3 It's *your* birthday soon! Ask and answer the
questions with a partner.

> *What would you like?*

> *I'd like a CD.*

> *I'd like a new car!*

> *What would you like to do on your birthday?*

> *I'd like to go out for dinner.*

> *I'd like to have a party.*

Talking about you

4 Work with a partner. Ask and answer the questions.

- Do you like traveling?
- Where do you like going?
- Where would you like to go next?
- Would you like to live in another country?
- Would you like to live in England?
- Do you like learning English?
- Would you like to learn more languages?

Why?/Why not?

> *Do you like traveling?*

> *Yes, I do./No, I don't.*

> *Where would you like to go next?*

> *I'd like to go to Thailand.*

GRAMMAR SPOT

1 We use *like* to talk about always.

I **like** coffee. I **don't like** tea. I **like** swimming.

2 We use *'d like* to talk about now or a time in the future.

I**'d like** a cup of coffee, please.
I**'d like** to go to Mexico next year.

▶▶ Grammar Reference 12.2 p. 129

Listening and pronunciation

5 **T 12.6** Put a check (✓) next to the sentence you hear.

1. ☐ Would you like a soda?
   ☐ Do you like soda?
2. ☐ I like orange juice.
   ☐ I'd like an orange juice.
3. ☐ We like going for walks.
   ☐ We'd like to go for a walk.
4. ☐ What do you like doing on the weekend?
   ☐ What would you like to do this weekend?
5. ☐ We'd like a new car.
   ☐ We like our new car.

Check it

6 Put a check (✓) next to the correct sentence.

1. ☐ I like to go home now, please.
   ☐ I'd like to go home now, please.
2. ☐ What would you like to do?
   ☐ What would you like do?
3. ☐ I like swimming.
   ☐ I'd like swimming.
4. ☐ You like a cup of coffee?
   ☐ Would you like a cup of coffee?
5. ☐ Do you like listen to music?
   ☐ Do you like listening to music?

VOCABULARY AND SPEAKING

In a restaurant

1 Match the food and photos. Write the words.

fish	cheese	salad	mineral water	soup
vegetables	chicken	fries	tomato	fruit

T 12.7 Listen and repeat.

1 cheese

2

3

4

5

6

7

8

9

10

2 Complete the menu with the words.

coffee   roast chicken

cheese   tomato juice   apple pie

salad   mineral water

cheeseburger

Joe's DINER

★★★★★★★

To start
chicken soup
tomato juice

Burgers
hamburger, salad, and fries
_____, salad, and fries

Sandwiches
tuna
chicken
_____

Meat
steak and salad
_____ and salad

Side orders
fries
_____

Desserts
ice cream
chocolate cake
_____

To drink
soda
orange juice
_____
_____

3 **T 12.8** Listen to Andrea and Paul ordering a meal in Joe's Diner. Who says these things? Write *W*, *A*, or *P*.

W = the waiter   A = Andrea   P = Paul

- [P] Andrea, what would you like to start?
- [ ] Can I have the tomato juice, please?
- [ ] And I'd like the chicken soup.
- [ ] Can I have the steak, please?
- [ ] How would you like it cooked?
- [ ] What would you like to drink?
- [ ] We'd like a bottle of mineral water, too.
- [ ] Delicious, thank you.

4 Look at the tapescript on p. 122. Practice the conversation in groups of three.

5 Have more conversations in Joe's Diner. Use the menu.

READING
She only eats junk food

1 Look at the words.
What food is good for you?

2 What's your favorite food?
Tell the class.

 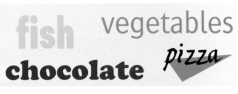

3 Read the newspaper article. What's unusual about Mary Alston?

BURGER QUEEN
She's 109 years old, and she only eats junk food.

Yesterday was Mary Alston's birthday. She is 109 years old, and she is the oldest person in the world. And she only eats junk food.

Mrs. Alston had a party with six generations of her family. Her daughter, Jenny Morgan, who is 85, said, "My mother loves chocolate, and eats only popcorn, pizzas, and burgers. She never eats fresh food. She says she doesn't like it."

Mrs. Alston lives in Harrisburg, Pennsylvania. She was born on a farm in Pennsylvania, and worked as a teacher. In 1915 she married James Henry Alston. He died in 1983.

Her granddaughter, Annie, who is 65, said, "Grandma gets up every day at six o'clock, and goes to the hairdresser every Friday."

Annie asked her grandmother what she wanted to eat on her birthday. Mary said, "I'd like a cheeseburger and fries!"

4 Match the questions and answers. Complete the sentences.

Questions	Answers
1. When was Mary Alston's birthday?	a. She was _____ teacher.
2. _____ she have a party?	b. She gets up at six o'clock.
3. Does she eat fresh food?	c. It ___was___ yesterday.
4. What _____ she eat?	d. "I _____ a cheeseburger and fries!"
5. What was her job?	e. Yes, she did.
6. _____ was she born?	f. She _____ to the hairdresser.
7. When did she marry?	g. Popcorn, pizza, and burgers.
8. What time does she _____ up?	h. No, she _____.
9. Where does she go every Friday?	i. On a farm in Pennsylvania.
10. What did she say to her granddaughter?	j. She married _____ 1915.

T 12.9 Listen and check. Practice the questions and answers with a partner.

EVERYDAY ENGLISH
Going shopping

1 **T 12.10** Listen to the conversations in different places. Use the words to complete the conversations.

In the street

1. **A** Excuse me! *Where can I buy film*
for my camera?
B In a drugstore.
A _____?
B Yes, 200 meters from here,
_____.

| can film Where I buy |
| there a Is drugstore here near |
| bank the to next |

In a clothing store

2. **A** Can I help you?
B _____. I'm just
looking.

| thanks No, |

3. **A** Excuse me! _____
in a medium?
B No, I'm sorry. _____.

| have shirt Do you this |
| all we That's have |

4. **A** _____ a pair
of jeans, please.
B Sure. _____?
A I think I'm a 26.
B OK. The fitting rooms are over
there.

| try like to I'd on |
| are size What you |

At the market

5. **A** Yes, miss. _____?
B _____
potatoes, please.
A Anything else?
B _____,
thanks. How much is that?

| like you would What |
| kilo a like I'd of |
| that's No, all |

At a newsstand

6. **A** Excuse me! _____
newspapers?
B _____, we
don't.
A Where _____?
B Try the hotel.

| Korean sell Do you |
| sorry No, I'm |
| them buy can I |

2 Work with a partner. Have similar conversations. You want these things.

Student A
- a birthday card
- this sweater (small/medium/large)
- apples
- pens

Student B
- a phone card
- this T-shirt (small/medium/large)
- tomatoes
- computer magazines

 **Grammar Reference 12.3 p. 129**

13

Here and now

STARTER

1 Look at the pictures of George and Sadie. Find the colors.

George

Sadie

black
white
red
blue
green
gray
yellow
brown

2 Complete the sentences with the colors.

1. George's jacket is ___black___. Sadie's jacket is _____.
2. His pants are _____. Her pants are _____.
3. Her shirt is _____. His shirt is _____.
4. Her shoes are _____. His shoes are _____.

T 13.1 Listen and check. Practice the sentences.

3 What colors are your clothes today?

WORK AND VACATIONS
Present Continuous

1 Read about George's job. Complete the text with the verbs.

goes   has   works   reads   enjoys   starts   leaves   wears

George _works_ in a bank. He _____ work at 9:00 and he _____ work at 5:00. He always _____ a black jacket and gray pants. He _____ lunch at 1:00. He sometimes _____ to the park and _____ his newspaper. He _____ his job.

2 **T 13.2** Listen and read about George on vacation.

Now George is on vacation in Thailand with his wife. He's wearing a white T-shirt. His wife is reading a book. They're having lunch. "We're having a great vacation," says George.

3 **T 13.3** Listen and repeat.

He's wearing a T-shirt.   She's reading a book.
They're having lunch.   We're having a great vacation.

4 Make true sentences about George's vacation.

George		swimming.
His wife		reading the menu.
Four people	is	playing tennis.
Two people	are	enjoying our vacation.
They		having lunch.
We		wearing a blue T-shirt.

▶▶ Grammar Reference 13.1 p. 130

GRAMMAR SPOT

1 George **is wearing** a white T-shirt. He**'s having** lunch.

These sentences say what George is doing *now*. This is the Present Continuous tense.

2 We make the Present Continuous with *am/are/is* + verb + *-ing*.

3 Complete the sentences using the verbs.

I	_am_	_studying_	English. (study)
You			jeans. (wear)
She			a book. (read)
We			in class. (work)
They			lunch. (have)

PRACTICE

Speaking

1 Work with a partner. What are these people doing?

I. He's cooking.

T 13.4 Listen and check.

2 Think of actions you can mime to your partner. Can your partner guess what you are doing?

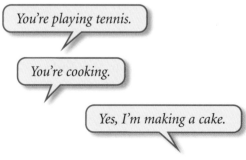

You're playing tennis.

You're cooking.

Yes, I'm making a cake.

I'M WORKING
Questions and negatives

1 **T 13.5** Read and listen to a radio interview with the model, Sadie.

WFAS 105.9FM
transcript

Fashion Spot 3:00 P.M. 09/17 [**I** – Interviewer, **S** – Sadie]

I What are you doing here in New York, Sadie?
S I'm working. There is a big fashion show here.
I Are you staying in a hotel?
S No, I'm not. I'm staying with friends.
I Are you having a good time in New York?
S Yes, I am. I'm enjoying it very much.
I Well Sadie, tell the listeners. What are you wearing now?
S I'm not wearing anything special! I'm just wearing jeans and a T-shirt.
I Thank you, Sadie. It was nice to talk to you.
S Thank you.

2 Ask and answer the questions with *she*.

1. What ... doing in New York?
2. Where ... staying?
3. ... having a good time?
4. What ... wearing?

> *What's she doing in New York?*

> *She's working.*

GRAMMAR SPOT

Present Continuous

1 Questions
What are you wearing?
Where's she staying?

2 Negatives
I'm not staying in a hotel.
He isn't working.
We aren't having breakfast.

3 Short answers
Are they having a good time? Yes, they are.
Are you working? No, I'm not.

▶▶ **Grammar Reference 13.2 and 13.3 p. 130**

PRACTICE

Asking questions

1 Look at the answers. Write the questions. Use the verbs.

read

What are you reading?

A love story.

1

watch

The news.

2

go

To my bedroom.

3

T 13.6 Listen and check.

wear

Because I'm cold.

4

eat

Chocolate.

5

make

Five.

6

talk to

My girlfriend.

7

2 Write the questions.

1. you / wear / a new sweater?
2. we / study / Chinese?
3. we / sit / in our classroom?
4. you / wear / new shoes?
5. the teacher / wear / blue pants?
6. it / rain?
7. all the students / speak / English?
8. you / learn / a lot of English?

Stand up. Ask and answer the questions.

Are you wearing a new sweater?

Yes, I am.

Are we studying Chinese?

No, we aren't. We're studying English.

Check it

3 Put a check (✓) next to the correct sentence.

1. ☐ I'm wear a blue shirt today.
   ☐ I'm wearing a blue shirt today.
2. ☐ Where are you going?
   ☐ Where you going?
3. ☐ Peter no working this week.
   ☐ Peter isn't working this week.
4. ☐ That's Peter over there. He talks to the teacher.
   ☐ That's Peter over there. He's talking to the teacher.
5. ☐ Michiko is Japanese. She comes from Osaka.
   ☐ Michiko is Japanese. She's coming from Osaka.

READING AND SPEAKING
Today's different

1 What do you usually do on Saturday? On your birthday? On New Year's Day? On Sunday evening?

2 Read one of the texts. Match a photograph 1–4 with your text.

3 Answer the questions.
1. What does he/she usually do on this day?
2. Why is today different?
3. What is he/she doing?
4. What happened this morning?
5. What is he/she wearing?
6. What are the people in the photographs doing?

4 Work in groups of four. Tell the others about your person. Use your answers in Exercise 3.

A photo of me

Bring a photograph of you to class. Say ...
- where you are
- what you're doing
- who you're with
- what you're wearing

Isabel

"On Saturday mornings I usually get up late and do housework. Then I meet some friends in town for lunch and go shopping in the afternoon."

But this Saturday is different! This morning Isabel got up early because today she's getting married. She's in church with all her family and friends. She's wearing a white dress, and her husband is standing next to her.

Leo

"On my birthday I sometimes go out with friends, or I go out to a restaurant with my family. My mom usually makes me a birthday cake."

But this birthday is different! It's Leo's eighteenth birthday, so now he's an adult. This morning he got a lot of presents. Now he's watching a movie with his friends. They're laughing and having a good time. Leo's wearing a white T-shirt.

Mark

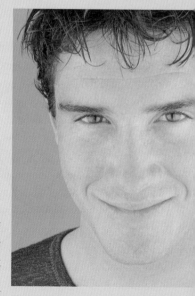

"On New Year's day we usually all go to my parents' house. We have a big lunch at about 3:00 in the afternoon."

But this New Year's day is different! Mark and his wife are in Australia, they're visiting friends. This morning they went swimming and now they're having a barbecue on the beach. It's hot and they're wearing their bathing suits.

Alissa

"I usually hate **Sunday evenings** because I don't like Mondays. I do my homework and get ready for school."

But this Sunday evening is different! Alissa's getting ready to go on a ski trip tomorrow. This morning she went to a friend's house, then she had lunch with her grandparents. Now she's packing her bags. She's trying on her ski clothes. She's enjoying this Sunday evening.

VOCABULARY AND SPEAKING
Clothes

1 Match the clothes and the photos. Write the words.

a shirt	boots	a skirt	shorts	a sweater
shoes	sandals	pants	a dress	a jacket
sneakers	a coat	a hat	a tie	socks

T 13.7 Listen and repeat. Which two items of clothing are only for women?

2 Say what the people are wearing.

> She's wearing a red and black skirt and a gray sweater.

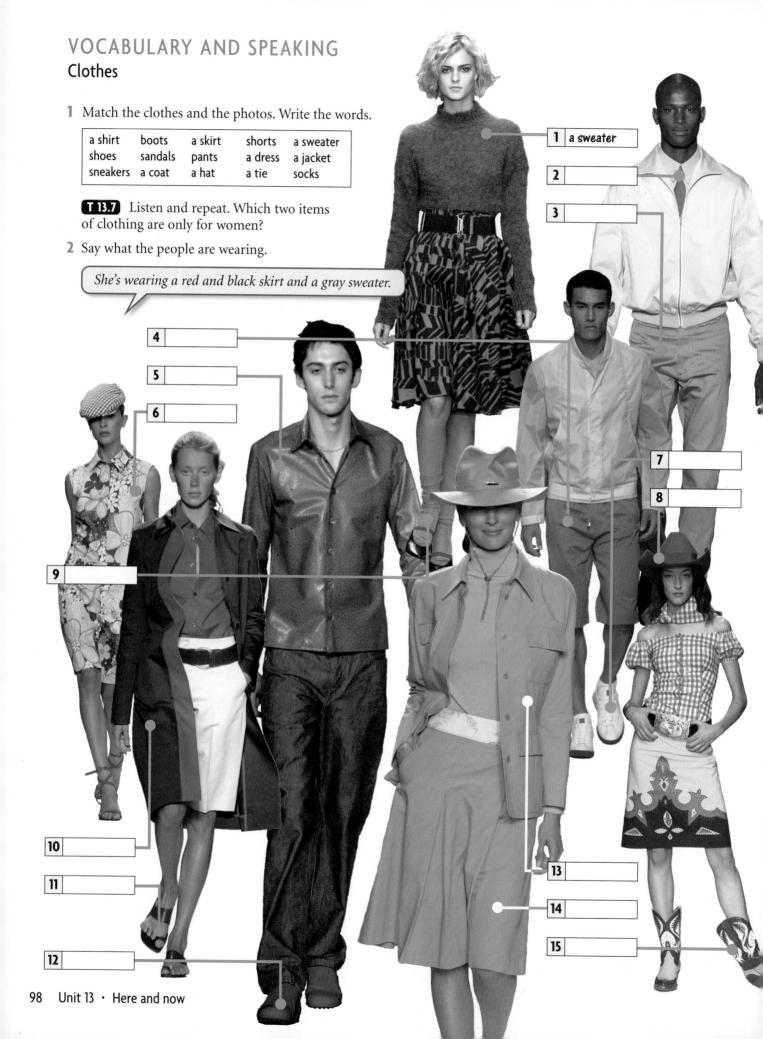

1 | a sweater

2 |

3 |

4 |

5 |

6 |

7 |

8 |

9 |

10 |

11 |

12 |

13 |

14 |

15 |

3 Stand back to back with another student. Ask questions to find out what he/she is wearing.

Are you wearing jeans?

No, I'm not.

Are you wearing pants?

Yes, I am.

Are they black?

Yes, they are.

4 Practice with a partner. Ask and answer the questions.

- What are your favorite colors?
- What are your favorite clothes?
- What do you wear during the week?
- What about on the weekend?

5 **T 13.8** Listen and complete the sentences with these words.

| eyes   short   brown   blonde |

1. She has long, _____ hair.
2. He has _____, black hair.
3. She has blue _____.
4. He has _____ eyes.

6 Describe a person in the room, but don't say who it is. Can the other students guess who it is?

She has brown hair and brown eyes. She's wearing … , and she's sitting …

Getting Information

7 Work with a partner.

Student A Go to page 113.
Student B Go to page 115.

EVERYDAY ENGLISH
What's the matter?

1 What's the matter with the people? Complete the sentences with these words.

| tired   hungry   thirsty   cold   hot   bored |

1 She's *cold.*

2 He's

3 They're

4 He's

5 They're

6 She's

T 13.9 Listen and repeat.

2 **T 13.10** Listen to the conversation. Practice with a partner.

A What's the matter?
B I'm tired and thirsty.
A Why don't you have a cup of coffee?
B That's a good idea.

3 Have similar conversations. Use these ideas.

- go to bed early
- have a cold drink
- sit down and relax
- put on a sweater
- go for a swim
- go to the movies
- have a sandwich
- watch a video
- take a shower

14 It's time to go!

Present Continuous for future · Question word review · Transportation and travel · Sightseeing

STARTER

1 What year is it? What year is it next year?
What month is it? What month is it next month?
What day is it today? What day is it tomorrow?

2 Say the months of the year and the days of the week around the class.

VACATION PLANS

Present Continuous for future

1 **T 14.1** Listen to Elena and read her diary for next week.
Why is she excited?

APRIL

6 Monday
pick up tickets from
the travel agent's

7 Tuesday
meet Grant and Nickie after work
go shopping

8 Wednesday
11:00 a.m. see the doctor
have lunch with Mom

9 Thursday
leave work early
pack bags

10 Friday
6:30 a.m. go by taxi to the airport
meet Grant and Nickie
9:30 a.m. fly to Mexico!

11 Saturday

12 Sunday

APRIL
M T W T F S S
1 2 3 4 5
6 7 8 9 10 11 12
13 14 15 16 17 18 19
20 21 22 23 24 25 26
27 28 29 30

2 Complete the sentences about Elena.

1. On Monday she's picking up her
   __tickets__ from the travel agent's.
2. On Tuesday she's meeting Grant and
   Nickie after _____ and they're
   going _____.
3. On Wednesday she's seeing the
   _____ at 11 o'clock, then she's
   _____ lunch with her mother.
4. On Thursday she's _____ work
   early and she's _____ her bags.
5. On Friday at 6:30 in the morning she's
   going by _____ to the airport
   and she's _____ Grant and
   Nickie there. At 9:30 they're
   _____ to Mexico.

GRAMMAR SPOT

1 The Present Continuous can express
future plans.

I'm going to Mexico next week.
She's seeing the doctor on Wednesday.
We're leaving next Friday.

2 We often say when *(this afternoon,
tomorrow, on Saturday, . . .)* with the
Present Continuous. Underline the time
expressions in Grammar Spot **1**.

▶▶ **Grammar Reference 14.1 p. 130**

Questions

3 ▪T 14.2▪ Listen and repeat the question
and answer.

What's she doing on Monday?
She's picking up her tickets.

Ask and answer more questions about
Elena's week. Work with a partner.

*What's she doing
on Tuesday?*

She's …

4 Write your diary for the next four days.
Ask and answer questions with a partner.

What are you doing tomorrow?

*I'm meeting my friends.
What are **you** doing?*

---

5 Look at the picture. It's Monday morning. Elena's at work. What's she
doing? Complete the conversation with the question words.

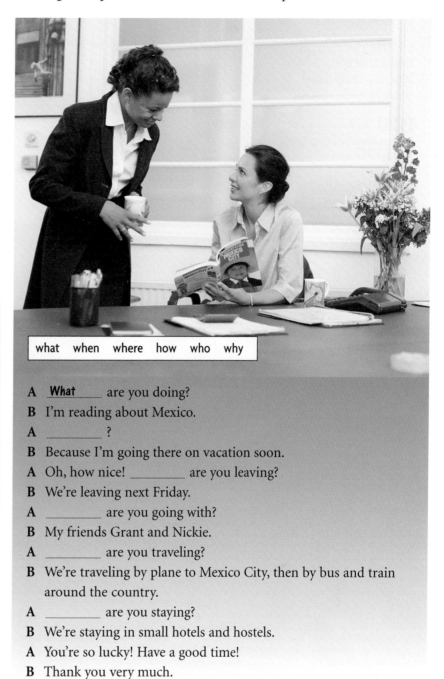

what	when	where	how	who	why

A __What__ are you doing?
B I'm reading about Mexico.
A _____?
B Because I'm going there on vacation soon.
A Oh, how nice! _____ are you leaving?
B We're leaving next Friday.
A _____ are you going with?
B My friends Grant and Nickie.
A _____ are you traveling?
B We're traveling by plane to Mexico City, then by bus and train
around the country.
A _____ are you staying?
B We're staying in small hotels and hostels.
A You're so lucky! Have a good time!
B Thank you very much.

▪T 14.3▪ Listen and check. Practice with a partner.

GRAMMAR SPOT

1 We make the question form with *When* and *I / you / he / she / we / they*.
When am I leaving?   When are you leaving?   When is he . . . ?

2 The Present Continuous can express the present and the future.
Which sentence is about now? Which sentence is about the future?
I'm reading about Mexico.   I'm leaving next Friday.

▶▶ **Grammar Reference 14.1 p. 130**

PRACTICE

Listening and speaking

1 Look at the chart about Marco's vacation plans. Write the questions.

Where is he going?
Why is he going there?
When . . . ?

T 14.4 Listen and check the questions. Complete the chart about Marco's vacation plans.

2 Ask and answer the questions about Marco with a partner.

Marco

Where / go?	Banff, Canada
Why / go?	to go skiing
When / leave?	
How / travel?	
Where / stay?	Banff Springs Hotel
How long / stay?	

Where's he going?

He's going to Banff in Canada.

3 Look at the pictures. Where are the people going on vacation, do you think?

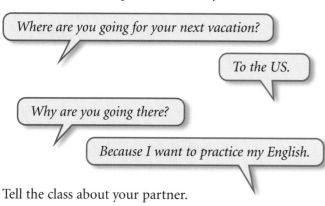

Work with a partner.

Student A Look at p. 111. Read about Rachel and Laura's vacation plans.
Student B Look at p. 113. Read about Omar's vacation plans.

Ask and answer the questions to complete your chart.

4 Ask and answer the questions about you.

> *Where are you going for your next vacation?*

> *To the US.*

> *Why are you going there?*

> *Because I want to practice my English.*

Tell the class about your partner.

> *Jun is going to the US because she wants to practice her English. She's ...*

Talking about you

5 Read the sentences about yesterday and ask a question about tomorrow.

Yesterday	Tomorrow
1. I got up early.	*Are you getting up early tomorrow?*
2. I went swimming.	*Are you going ... ?*
3. I walked to work.	
4. I had lunch in my office.	
5. I left work late.	
6. I met a friend.	
7. We had dinner in a restaurant.	

T 14.5 Listen, check, and repeat. Practice the intonation in the questions.

6 Write what you did yesterday. Tell a partner. Ask and answer questions about tomorrow.

> *I went to my English class.*

> *Are you going to your English class tomorrow?*

> *No, I'm not. I'm ...*

Check it

7 Put a check (✓) next to the correct sentence.
1. ☐ I'm leaving tomorrow.
   ☐ I leaving tomorrow.
2. ☐ We go to the movies this evening.
   ☐ We're going to the movies this evening.
3. ☐ Where they go on vacation?
   ☐ Where are they going on vacation?
4. ☐ Where are you doing on Saturday evening?
   ☐ What are you doing on Saturday evening?
5. ☐ What do you do tomorrow?
   ☐ What are you doing tomorrow?

READING AND LISTENING
A musical trip around the US

1 **T 14.6** Listen to three pieces of music and look at the pictures.
Match the picture and the music. Which US city is famous for which type of music?

Memphis   **New Orleans**   **Nashville**

2 **T 14.7** Read and listen about two friends who are going on a trip to the US next month.
Where are they from? What is special about their trip? Write the cities they are visiting on the map.

Rocking Around the US!

Noboru Hideki and Roku Ito are Japanese. They're from Tokyo and they are crazy about American music. They go to concerts all over Japan, but next month they're going to the US. They're taking a road trip from one home of jazz to another—from Louisiana in the south to New York in the north. They're starting in New Orleans during Jazz Fest Week.

"It's so exciting," says Roku. "We're staying in the noisy French Quarter of the city."

From there, they're driving north to Memphis, Tennessee, the home of Elvis Presley. There, they're visiting Elvis's house, Graceland, which has more visitors than the White House.

"We're staying at a motel. It has a 24-hour Elvis movie channel in every room! It's fantastic!" says Noboru.

After Memphis, Tennessee, it's Nashville, Tennessee. There they want to listen to live country music in some of the small clubs.

"But Roku prefers rock and roll so we're staying just two days and then going to Cleveland, because this is where rock 'n roll got its name. A DJ there named it on his radio show in 1951."

They're finishing their trip in New York City. "So many musicians love playing in New York. We're visiting some of the jazz clubs. There are a lot of jazz clubs in Harlem and Greenwich Village. We can't wait. It's the trip of our dreams!"

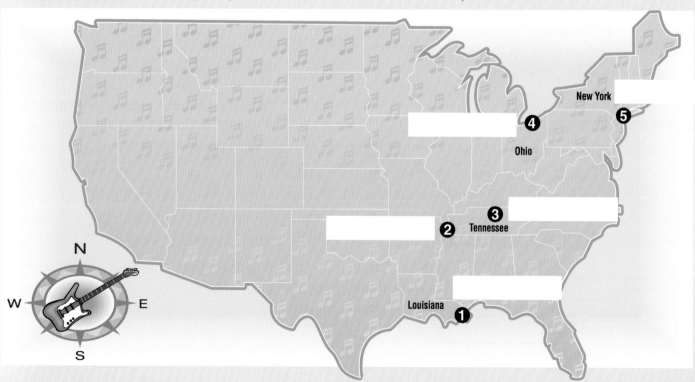

3 Correct the sentences about the text.

1. Noboru and Roku don't like American music.
   They're crazy about American music.

2. They went to the US last month.
   _____

3. They're traveling from the north to the south.
   _____

4. Elvis Presley's house is in Nashville, Tennessee.
   _____

5. They are visiting the White House.
   _____

6. Roku likes country music more than rock 'n roll.
   _____

7. A DJ in Cleveland named rock 'n roll in 1961.
   _____

8. There aren't many jazz clubs in Harlem.
   _____

4 Work with a partner and use the cities on the map to talk about Noboru and Roku's trip.

First, they're going to New Orleans because they want to …

Next, they're … because

Then, …

Finally, …

5 **T 14.8** Listen to a song by a famous American singer and songwriter Woody Guthrie. It's called "This Land Is Your Land."

How many lines and words can you remember? Tell the class. Turn to p. 123. Listen again and read the words of the song.

Sing about your land!

6 Work in groups. Write a similar song about your country. What places do you want to include?

Begin: This land is my land, this land is your land

…

End: This land was made for you and me.

Sing it to the class!

VOCABULARY AND SPEAKING

Transportation and travel

1 Match the transportation and photos.

> bicycle ship the subway motorcycle

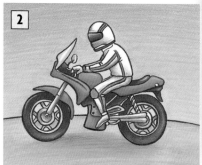

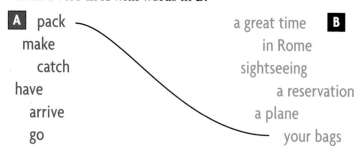

2 Work with a partner. How many other forms of transportation do you know?

3 Match a verb in **A** with words in **B**.

A	**B**
pack	a great time
make	in Rome
catch	sightseeing
have	a reservation
arrive	a plane
go	your bags

4 Put the sentences in the correct order.

- 1 We wanted to go on vacation to Rome.
- ☐ We caught the plane.
- ☐ We went to the airport.
- ☐ We made a reservation for the hotel and the flight.
- ☐ We packed our bags.
- ☐ We arrived in Rome.
- ☐ We picked up our tickets from the travel agent's.
- ☐ We went sightseeing.
- 9 We had a great time.

T 14.9 Listen and check.

5 Describe a trip in the past.

Where did you go? How did you travel? How long was the trip?

EVERYDAY ENGLISH
Going sightseeing

1 Write down the names of two cities and the dates when you were a tourist there.

London, July 2000.   Bangkok, January 2002.

Show a partner. Talk about the cities. What did you do there? What did you see? What did you buy?

- I went to . . .
- I saw . . .
- We visited . . .
- I bought . . .

2 **T 14.10** Listen and complete the conversations in a tourist office.

1. **A** Hi. Can I __help__ __you__?
   B Yes. _____ _____ a map of the city, please.
   A _____ you are.
   B Thank you.

2. **C** We'd like _____ _____ _____ a bus tour of _____ _____.
   A OK. The next _____ _____ at 10:00. It _____ an hour.
   C Where does the bus leave from?
   A It _____ _____ the _____ _____ on Maple Street.

3. **D** We'd like to visit the museum. _____ _____ _____ open?
   A From nine o'clock to five o'clock _____ _____.
   D _____ _____ is it to get in?
   A Ten dollars for adults and _____ _____ for children.

Practice the conversations.

3 What is there to do in your town? Where do visitors go?

> We have a beautiful park.

> There's a museum.

> Visitors go to the market/ the old town . . .

Work with a partner. One of you works in the Tourist Office in your town. The other is a tourist who wants some information.

A Hello. I'd like to go on a tour of the town/see the museum . . .
B OK. . . .

Getting Information

Cities and countries

2 Ask your partner questions and write the answers to complete the information.

> What's her name?

> Where's she from?

Her name's Carol.
She's from London.

Her name's Paula.
She's from Rio de Janeiro.

Her name's Rosa. She's
from Mexico City.

His name's Doug. He's
from Toronto.

Role play

5 Work in pairs. Read your role card. Ask and answer questions to complete the chart for your partner.

Man	
Name	Rodrigo Lutello
City, Country	Rio de Janeiro, Brazil
House or apartment	house
Job	doctor
Place of work	hospital
Languages	3 – Portuguese, Spanish, and English
Sports	skiing and basketball

Woman	
Name	Akemi Tanaka
City, Country	Tokyo, Japan
House or apartment	apartment
Job	teacher
Place of work	school in the center of town
Languages	2 – Japanese and English
Sports	tennis and swimming

What . . . ?
How do you spell it?

Where . . . live?

Do . . . live in . . . ?

What . . . do?

Where . . . work?

How many . . . speak?

What sports . . . like?

... about you

Name	
City, Country	
A house or an apartment	
Job	
Place of work	
Languages	
Sports	

Getting information

3 Work with a partner. Ask and answer questions to complete the clocks.

Student A   What time does he get up?
Student B   He gets up at six twenty. What time does he …?

1	2	3	4	5	6
get up	get home from school	get home from work	have dinner	get home from English class	go to bed

Student B

Role play

5 Work in pairs. Read your role card. Ask and answer questions to complete the chart for your partner.

Man	
Name	Young-soo Lee
City, Country	Seoul, Korea
House or apartment	house
Job	teacher
Place of work	school in the center of town
Languages	3 – Korean, English, and a little Chinese
Sports	skiing and baseball

Woman	
Name	Laura Gomez
City, Country	Mexico City, Mexico
House or apartment	apartment
Job	doctor
Place of work	hospital
Languages	Spanish, English, and a little French
Sports	tennis and swimming

What . . . ?
How do you spell it?

Where . . . live?

Do . . . live in . . . ?

What . . . do?

Where . . . work?

How many . . . speak?

What sports . . . like?

... *about you*

Name	
City, Country	
A house or an apartment	
Job	
Place of work	
Languages	
Sports	

Student B

Getting information

3 Work with a partner. Ask and answer questions to complete the clocks.

Student A   What time does he get up?
Student B   He gets up at six twenty. What time does he …?

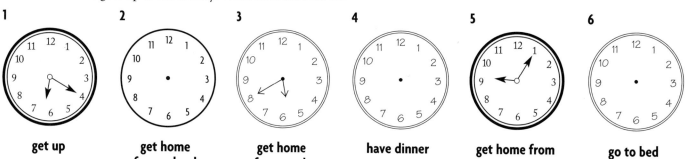

1	2	3	4	5	6
get up	get home from school	get home from work	have dinner	get home from English class	go to bed

Different rooms

3 Look at the picture of a room. Your partner has a different room. Talk about your pictures to find six differences.

In my picture, there's a …

In my picture, there isn't a …

Is there a … ?

No, there isn't.

Listening and speaking

3 Read about Rachel and Laura's vacation plans. Answer questions about Rachel and Laura. Ask your partner questions about Omar. Complete the chart.

Where is Omar going?

Why is he going there?

Rachel + Laura   Omar

Where / go?	Whangaparada, New Zealand	
Why / go?	to visit their uncle	
When / leave?	December 22	
How / travel?	by plane and car	
Where / stay?	their uncle's house	
How long / stay?	3 weeks	

Getting information

4 Look at Jane's apartment. What did she do yesterday? Answer questions about Jane. Ask your partner questions about Paul's day.

> **Student A** What sport did Paul play yesterday?
>
> **Student B** He played soccer. What did Jane do yesterday?

What sport/Paul/play/yesterday?
What/he/read?
Where/he/play the guitar?

Paul/cook dinner?
he/watch a video?
he/take a bath?
he/work on his computer

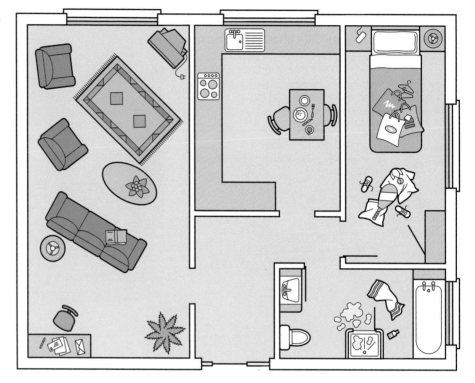

Getting information

8 Work in pairs to complete the dialogue with the correct form of *listen to, play, book, watch,* or *read.* Use the Present Simple and Past Simple.

A Did you have a good weekend?

B Yes, I _____**played**_____ tennis with my brother on Saturday, and yesterday I
(1) _____ my favorite movie on video. What about you?

A I (2) <u>booked</u> my summer vacation on the Internet—two weeks in Alaska.

B Really? That's interesting. Do you use your computer a lot?

A Oh, yes, every day. I (3) _____ computer games, (4) <u>listen to</u> music,
and (5) _____ newspapers.

B Can you (6) <u>book</u> theater tickets on the Internet? I want to see a new play
in New York.

A Yes, of course. It's easy. I can show you.

B OK. Thanks.

Practice the dialogue with your partner.

Getting information

7 Look at the picture of a family. Your partner has a different picture of the same family. There are six differences. Talk about the pictures to find them. Don't look at your partner's picture.

In my picture, the mother is listening …

In my picture, the mother is …

Listening and speaking

3 Read about Omar's vacation plans. Answer questions about Omar. Ask your partner questions about Rachel and Laura. Complete the chart.

Where is Rachel and Laura going?

Why are they going there?

Rachel + Laura   Omar

Where / go?		South Africa
Why / go?		to go on safari
When / leave?		next Saturday
How / travel?		by plane from Boston to Cape Town, then by jeep
Where / stay?		in hotels and tent
How long / stay?		2 weeks

Getting information

4 Look at Paul's apartment. What did he do yesterday? Answer questions about Paul. Ask your partner questions about Jane's day.

Student A What sport did Paul play yesterday?

Student B He played soccer. What did Jane do yesterday?

Where/Jane/go/yesterday?
What/she/read?
What sport/Jane/play/yesterday?

Jane/have breakfast?
she/write a letter?
she/take a shower?
she/watch TV

Getting information

8 Work in pairs to complete the dialogue with the correct form of *listen to, play, book, watch,* or *read.* Use the Present Simple and Past Simple.

A Did you have a good weekend?

B Yes, I _____**played**_____ tennis with my brother on Saturday, and yesterday I (1) <u>watched</u> my favorite movie on video. What about you?

A I (2) _____ my summer vacation on the Internet—two weeks in Alaska.

B Really? That's interesting. Do you use your computer a lot?

A Oh, yes, every day. I (3) <u>play</u> computer games, (4) _____ music, and (5) <u>read</u> newspapers.

B Can you (6) _____ theater tickets on the Internet? I want to see a new play in New York.

A Yes, of course. It's easy. I can show you.

B OK. Thanks.

Practice the dialogue with your partner.

Getting information

7 Look at the picture of a family. Your partner has a different picture of the same family. There are six differences. Talk about the pictures to find them. Don't look at your partner's picture.

In my picture, the mother is listening …

In my picture, the mother is …

Tapescripts

Unit 1

T 1.1 see p. 2

T 1.2 see p. 2

T 1.3 see p. 3

T 1.4 see p. 4

T 1.5 see p. 4

T 1.6 Introductions
1. **A** Hello. My name's Anna. What's your name?
   B Ben.
2. **C** Hi. My name's Carla. What's your name?
   D My name's Dennis.

T 1.7
1. **B** Hi, Anna. How are you?
   A Fine, thanks, Ben. And you?
   B Fine, thanks.
2. **D** Hi, Carla. How are you?
   C Fine, thanks. And you?
   D OK, thanks.

T 1.8
P Hi. My name's Pam. What's your name?
T I'm Tina, and this is Mary.
P Hi, Tina. Hi, Mary.
M Hi, Pam. How are you?
P I'm OK, thanks. And you?
M Fine, thanks.

T 1.9 see p. 6

T 1.10 see p. 6

T 1.11 see p. 7

T 1.12 Listen and check
a. ten sandwiches
b. two books
c. six bags
d. five computers
e. four houses
f. seven hamburgers
g. eight cameras
h. nine photographs
i. three cars
j. ten students

T 1.13 see p. 7

Unit 2

T 2.1 see p. 8

T 2.2 see p. 8

T 2.3 see p. 8

T 2.4 Where are you from?
1. Her name's Jenny.
   She's from Canada.
2. His name's Rick.
   He's from the United States.
3. Her name's Bianca.
   She's from Brazil.
4. His name's Jack.
   He's from England.
5. Her name's Jun.
   She's from Korea.
6. His name's Fu-an.
   He's from Taiwan.
7. Her name's Kim.
   She's from Australia.

T 2.5 see p. 9

T 2.6 Cities and countries
Where's Tokyo?   It's in Japan.
Where's Seoul?   It's in Korea.
Where's Toronto?   It's in Canada.
Where's Rio de Janeiro? It's in Brazil.
Where's London?   It's in England.
Where's Boston?   It's in the United States.
Where's Sydney?   It's in Australia.
Where's Mexico City?   It's in Mexico.

T 2.7 Questions and answers
S Hi, I'm Sandra. What's your name?
L My name's Luis.
S Hi, Luis. Where are you from?
L I'm from Mexico. Where are *you* from?
S Oh, I'm from Mexico, too. I'm from Mexico City.

T 2.8 Listen and write
1. **G** Hello, I'm Gabriel. I'm from Brazil.
   A Hello, Gabriel. I'm Akemi from Japan.
2. **C** Hello. My name's Charles. What's your name?
   M Hi, Charles. I'm Mike. I'm from the United States. Where are *you* from?
   C I'm from London, in England.
   M Oh, yeah? I'm from Chicago.
3. **L** Hi, I'm Loretta. I'm from Sydney, Australia.
   J Hi, Loretta. I'm Jason. I'm from Australia, too.
   L Wow! Are you from Sydney?
   J No. I'm from Melbourne.

T 2.9 Listen and check
1. Where are you from?
   I'm from Brazil.
2. What's her name?
   Her name's Amina.
3. What's his name?
   His name's Luis.
4. Where's he from?
   He's from Mexico City.
5. What's this in English?
   It's a computer.
6. How are you?
   Fine, thanks.
7. Where's Toronto?
   It's in Canada.

T 2.10 see p. 12

T 2.11 see p. 13

T 2.12 Listen and repeat
twenty-one
twenty-two
twenty-three
twenty-four
twenty-five
twenty-six
twenty-seven
twenty-eight
twenty-nine
thirty

T 2.13 Listen and check
1. twelve
2. sixteen
3. twenty-one
4. seventeen
5. thirty

Unit 3

T 3.1 Jobs
1. a teacher
2. a taxi driver
3. a police officer
4. a businessman
5. a doctor
6. a sales assistant
7. a nurse
8. a student

T 3.2 see p. 14

T 3.3 see p. 14

T 3.4 Listen and check
1. What's her name?   Amy Roberts.
2. Where's she from?   The United States.
3. What's her address?   18 Cedar Street, Chicago.
4. What's her
   phone number?   It's (773) 726-6049.
5. How old is she?   She's 20.
6. What's her job?   She's a student.
7. Is she married?   No, she isn't.

T 3.5 see p. 15

T 3.6 Negatives and short answers
A Is your name Jeff?
B Yes, it is.
A Are you from England, Jeff?
B No, I'm not from England. I'm from Houston, Texas.
A Are you a police officer?
B Yes, I am.
A Are you 23?
B No, I'm not. I'm 25.
A Are you married?
B Yes, I am.

T 3.7 Listen to the conversations
Sang-hoon Pak
A Good morning.
B Hi.
A What's your name, please?
B My name's Sang-hoon Pak.
A Thank you. And where are you from, Sang-hoon?
B I'm from Seoul, in Korea.
A Thank you. And your telephone number, please?

B It's (822) 773-3862.
A How old are you, Sang-hoon?
B I'm 23.
A And … what's your job?
B I'm a businessman.
A And … are you married?
B No, I'm not.
A Thank you very much.

Diana Black
A Hello.
C Hi.
A What's your name, please?
C Diana Black.
A And where are you from?
C From New York.
A Ah! So you're from the United States?
C Yes, I am.
A What's your phone number?
C It's (646) 463-9145.
A Thank you. How old are you?
C I'm 29.
A What's your job, Ms. Black?
C I'm a sales assistant.
A Are you married?
C Yes, I am.
A OK. Thank you very much.

T 3.8 **A pop group**
I = Interviewer   Jen = Jennifer   Jas = Jason
M = Melanie   R = Robert
I Hi!
All Hi!
I Now you're Melanie, right?
M That's right.
I And you're from Australia.
M Uh-huh.
I How old are you, Melanie?
M I'm 22.
I And Jason and Jennifer. You're from England, right?
Jas No, no. We aren't from England. We're from the United States.
I The United States. Sorry. How old are you both?
Jen I'm 21 and Jason is 20.
R And I'm 19.
I Thanks. Now, who's married in 4 x 4?
R Well, I'm not married.
Jen and Jas We aren't married!
I Melanie, are you married?
M Yes, I am!
I Well, thank you, 4 x 4. Welcome to New York!
All It's great here. Thanks!

T 3.9 **Social expressions**
1. **A** Good morning.
   B Good morning, Mr. Brown.
2. **A** Good afternoon. The Grand Hotel.
   B Good afternoon.
3. **A** Good night.
   B Good night, Peter.
4. **A** Good-bye!
   B Good-bye! Have a good trip!

T 3.10 **Listen and complete**
1. **A** What's this in English?
   B I don't know.
   A It's a dictionary.
2. **A** *Hogy hívnak?*
   B Sorry. I don't understand.
   A What's your name?
   B My name's Manuel. I'm from Venezuela.

3. **A** The homework is on page … of the Workbook.
   B Excuse me?
   A The homework is on page *30* of the Workbook.
   B Thank you.

Unit 4

T 4.1 **Listen and check**
I, my
you, your
he, his
she, her
we, our
they, their

T 4.2 see p. 20

T 4.3 **Listen and check**
1. Is Patty married?
   Yes, she is.
2. Where's their house?
   It's in Los Angeles.
3. What is Patty's job?
   She's a teacher.
4. Where's her school?
   It's in the center of town.
5. What is Tom's job?
   He's a bank manager.
6. Where's his bank?
   It's in the center of town.
7. Are their children doctors?
   No, they aren't. They're students.

T 4.4 see p. 21

T 4.5 **Listen and check**
1. Patty is Tom's wife.
2. Tom is Patty's husband.
3. Kayla is Patty and Tom's daughter.
4. Nick is their son.
5. Patty is Nick's mother.
6. Tom is Kayla's father.
7. Kayla is Nick's sister.
8. Nick is Kayla's brother.
9. Patty and Tom are Kayla and Nick's parents.
10. Kayla and Nick are Tom and Patty's children.

T 4.6 **The family**
Hi! My name's Rachel, and I'm from the United States. This is a photo of my family. Our house is in San Diego. This is my brother. His name is Steve, and he's 15. He's a student in high school. This is my mother. Her name's Grace. She's 42, and she's a doctor. And this man is my father, Joe. He's 44, and he's a businessman.

T 4.7 see p. 23

T 4.8 **Listen and write**
1. I have a small farm in Vermont.
2. My wife has a job in town.
3. We have one son.
4. We have two dogs.
5. My sister and her husband have a house in Los Angeles.
6. He has a very good job.
7. They have a son and a daughter.

T 4.9 **Listen and check**
1. How is your mother?
   She's fine, thank you.
2. What's your sister's job?
   She's a nurse.
3. How old are your brothers?
   They're ten and thirteen.
4. Who is Patty?
   She's David's sister.
5. Where's your office?
   It's in the center of town.
6. Are you and your husband from Peru?
   Yes, we are.

T 4.10 see p. 26

T 4.11 **Write the names**
1. What's your name?
   Patty Milton.
   How do you spell your first name?
   P-a-t-t-y.
   How do you spell your last name?
   M-i-l-t-o-n.
2. What's your name?
   David Ruiz.
   How do you spell your first name?
   D-a-v-i-d.
   How do you spell your last name?
   R-u-i-z.
3. What's your name?
   Amtul Patel.
   How do you spell your first name?
   A-m-t-u-l.
   How do you spell your last name?
   P-a-t-e-l.
4. What's your name?
   Akiko Matsuda.
   How do you spell your first name?
   A-k-i-k-o.
   How do you spell your last name?
   M-a-t-s-u-d-a.
5. What's your name?
   Jun-hao Chen.
   How do you spell your first name?
   J-u-n-h-a-o.
   How do you spell your last name?
   C-h-e-n.

T 4.12 see p. 27

Unit 5

T 5.1 see p. 28

T 5.2 see p. 29

T 5.3 **Bill**
Well, I like swimming and basketball. I don't like tennis. Mmm … yeah, hamburgers and pizza—I like hamburgers and pizza. And Chinese food, I like Chinese food a lot—but not Italian food. I don't like Italian food and I don't like tea, but I like coffee and soda.

T 5.4 see p. 29

T 5.5 see p. 30

T 5.6 see p. 30

T 5.7 Listen and complete

W = woman   B = Brad
1. **W** Do you come from Ohio?
   B Yes, I do.
2. **W** Do you live in Cleveland?
   B No, I don't. I live in New York.
3. **W** Do you live in an apartment?
   B Yes, I do. I live in an apartment downtown.
4. **W** Do you work in a Chinese restaurant?
   B No, I don't. I work in an Italian restaurant.
5. **W** Do you like Italian food?
   B Yes, I do. I like it a lot.
6. **W** Do you like your job?
   B No, I don't. I want to be an actor.
7. **W** Do you drink tea?
   B No, I don't. I don't like it.
8. **W** Do you speak Spanish and German?
   B I speak Spanish, but I don't speak German.

T 5.8 see p. 31

T 5.9 Languages and nationalities

England	English
Italy	Italian
Spain	Spanish
Mexico	Mexican
Brazil	Brazilian
Japan	Japanese
China	Chinese
France	French
the United States	American
Korea	Korean

T 5.10 Listen and check

1. In Brazil they speak Portuguese.
2. In Canada they speak English and French.
3. In France they speak French.
4. In England they speak English.
5. In Italy they speak Italian.
6. In Japan they speak Japanese.
7. In Mexico they speak Spanish.
8. In Taiwan they speak Chinese.
9. In Spain they speak Spanish.
10. In Korea they speak Korean.
11. In the United States they speak English.

T 5.11 Listen and check

1. an American car
2. a Korean TV
3. Spanish oranges
4. a Japanese camera
5. Mexican food
6. an English dictionary
7. an Italian bag
8. Brazilian coffee
9. Chinese tea

T 5.12 At a party

A = Alessandra   J = Justin
A Hello. I'm Alessandra.
J Hi, Alessandra. I'm Justin. Justin Bates.
A Do you live here in Seattle, Justin?
J No, I don't. I work in Seattle, but I live in Tacoma.
A What do you do?
J I'm an actor. What do you do?
A I work in a hotel.
J You aren't American, but you speak English very well. Where do you come from?
A I'm Brazilian. I come from Rio.
J Oh, I love Brazil.
A Really?
J Oh, yes. I like the people and the food a lot.

T 5.13 see p. 35

T 5.14 see p. 35

T 5.15 see p. 35

T 5.16 Listen and check

1. The chicken sandwich is $3.90.
2. The baseball is $14.
3. The camera is $90.99.
4. The water is $1.50.
5. The chocolate is 60¢.
6. The cell phone is $24.74.
7. The dictionary is $16.95.
8. The bag is $30.99.

Unit 6

T 6.1 Listen and repeat

1. It's nine o'clock.
2. It's nine thirty.
3. It's nine forty-five.
4. It's ten o'clock.
5. It's ten fifteen.
6. It's two o'clock.
7. It's two thirty.
8. It's two forty-five.
9. It's three o'clock.
10. It's three fifteen.

T 6.2 see p. 36

T 6.3 Lena

Well, on weekdays I get up at seven forty-five. I have breakfast at eight and I go to school at eight thirty. I have lunch in school with my friends, that's at twelve fifteen—it's early in our school. I leave school at three thirty in the afternoon and I walk home with my friends. I get home at four thirty. I go to bed at eleven o'clock on weekdays but not on the weekend.

T 6.4 see p. 37

T 6.5 Listen and repeat

1. gets up
   takes a shower
2. has breakfast
3. leaves home
   goes to work
4. has lunch
5. works late
   leaves work
6. buys
   eats
   gets home
7. goes out
   works
8. goes to bed

T 6.6 Listen and repeat

He usually works late.
He sometimes buys a pizza.
He never goes out in the evening.

T 6.7 Questions and negatives

1. What time does he get up?
   He gets up at six o'clock.
2. When does he go to bed?
   He goes to bed at eleven forty-five.
3. Does he go to work by taxi?
   Yes, he does.
4. Does he have lunch in a restaurant?
   No, he doesn't.
5. Does he go out in the evening?
   No, he doesn't.

T 6.8 Listen and check

1. What time does he have breakfast?
   He has breakfast at six forty-five.
2. When does he leave home?
   He leaves home at seven fifteen.
3. Does he go to work by bus?
   No, he doesn't. He goes to work by taxi.
4. Where does he have lunch?
   He has lunch in his office.
5. Does he usually work late?
   Yes, he does.
6. Does he eat in a restaurant?
   No, he doesn't. He sometimes buys a pizza and eats it at home.
7. What does he do in the evening?
   He works on his computer.

T 6.9 Katya's day

Katya is 25. She's an artist. She lives in a small house in the country. She usually gets up at ten o'clock in the morning. She never gets up early. She has coffee and toast for breakfast and then she goes for a walk with her dog. She gets home at eleven o'clock and she paints in her studio until seven o'clock in the evening. Then she cooks dinner and drinks a cup of tea. After dinner, she sometimes listens to music and she sometimes plays the piano. She usually goes to bed very late, at one or two o'clock in the morning.

T 6.10 Negatives and pronunciation

1. She doesn't live in the city. She lives in the country.
2. He doesn't get up at ten o'clock. He gets up at six o'clock.
3. She doesn't have a big breakfast. She has coffee and toast.
4. He doesn't have a dog. She has a dog.
5. She doesn't work in an office. She works at home.
6. He doesn't cook dinner in the evening. He buys a pizza.
7. She doesn't go to bed early. She goes to bed late.
8. They don't go out in the evening. They stay home.

T 6.11 Words that go together

get up early
go to bed late
listen to music
watch TV
cook dinner
work in an office
go shopping
take a shower
eat in restaurants
drink water
play the piano
stay home

T 6.12 see p. 42

T 6.13 Days of the week

Monday
Tuesday
Wednesday
Thursday
Friday
Saturday
Sunday

T 6.14 Listen and check

on Sunday
on Monday
on Saturday evening
on Thursday morning
on Friday afternoon
on the weekend
at nine o'clock
at ten thirty
at twelve fifteen
in the morning
in the afternoon
in the evening

Unit 7

T 7.1 Listen and check

1. What is the capital of Australia?
   Canberra.
2. How old are the Pyramids?
   4,500 years old.
3. What time do Mexican people have dinner?
   Late. At 9:00 in the evening.
4. Where does the American president live?
   In the White House.
5. How many floors does the Empire State Building have?
   Eighty-six.
6. How much is a hamburger in the US?
   $3.50.
7. Who lives in Buckingham Palace?
   The queen of England.

T 7.2 I love it here!

C = Celine G = Gary

G This is a very beautiful house.
C Thank you. I like it very much, too.
G Celine, you're American. Why do you live here in London?
C Because I just love it here! The people are fantastic! I love them! And of course, my husband, Charles, is English, and I love him, too!
G That's a very nice photo. Who are they?
C My sons. That's Matt and that's Jack. They go to school here. My daughter's at school in the US. Her name's Lisa-Marie.
G Why does Lisa-Marie go to school in the US?
C Because she lives with her father. My first husband, you know—the actor Dan Brat. I hate him and all his movies. I never watch them.
G I see. So does Lisa-Marie visit you?
C Oh, yes. She visits me every vacation. She's here with me now.
G And is this a photo of you and Charles?
C Oh, yes. It's us in Hawaii. It's our wedding. We're so happy together!

T 7.3 I like them!

1. Do you like ice cream?
   Yes, I love it.

2. Do you like dogs?
   No, I hate them.
3. Do you like me?
   Of course I like you!
4. Does your teacher teach you Spanish?
   No, she teaches us English.
5. Do you like your teacher?
   We like her very much.

T 7.4 Questions and answers

1. Why does Celine drink tea?
   Because she likes it.
2. Why do you eat oranges?
   Because I like them.
3. Why does Annie want to marry Peter?
   Because she loves him.
4. Why do you eat Chinese food?
   Because I like it.
5. Why don't you like your math teacher?
   Because he gives us a lot of homework.
6. Why does Miguel buy presents for Maria?
   Because he loves her.

T 7.5 Listen and check

1. How do you come to school?
   By bus.
2. What do you have for breakfast?
   Toast and coffee.
3. Who is your favorite pop group?
   I don't have a favorite. I like a lot of groups.
4. Where does your father work?
   In an office in the center of town.
5. Why do you want to learn English?
   Because it's an international language.
6. How much money do you have?
   Not a lot. About two dollars.
7. When do classes start at your school?
   They start at nine o'clock.
8. How many languages does your teacher speak?
   Three.

T 7.6 Adjectives

1. It's great.
2. It's awful.
3. He's hot.
4. She's cold.
5. They're old.
6. They're new.
7. It's big.
8. It's small.
9. They're expensive.
10. They're cheap.

T 7.7 see p. 49

T 7.8 Listen to Keiko

1. A Next, please!
   K Can I have a tuna sandwich, please?
   A OK.
   K How much is that?
   A That's three ninety-five, please.
   K Here you are.
   A Thanks a lot.
2. K Hi. Can I try on this sweater, please?
   B Of course. The fitting rooms are over there.
3. K Can I send an e-mail, please?
   C OK. Computer number two.
   K How much is it?
   C Forty-five cents a minute. You pay at the end.

4. D Good morning. Can I help you?
   K Yes, please. Can I change a traveler's check?
   D How much is it?
   K Fifty dollars.
   D OK.
5. K Can I buy a round-trip ticket to Milford, please?
   E Sure.
   K How much is that?
   E Eighteen dollars, please.
   K Thank you.
   E Twenty dollars. Here's your ticket, and $2.00 change.

Unit 8

T 8.1 Listen and repeat

living room
dining room
kitchen
bathroom
bedroom

T 8.2 see p. 52

T 8.3 Janet's living room

My living room isn't very big, but I love it. There's a sofa, and there are two armchairs. There's a small table with a TV on it, and there are a lot of books. There's a CD player, and there are some CDs. There are pictures on the wall, and there are two lamps. It's a very comfortable room.

T 8.4 see p. 53

T 8.5 Prepositions

1. Janet's cell phone is on the bed.
2. The magazine is next to the phone.
3. Her CD player is on the floor next to the desk.
4. Her car keys are in the drawer.
5. Her bag is on the floor under the chair.
6. The books are under her bed.

T 8.6 Listen and check

1. Do you live in a house or an apartment?
2. How many bedrooms are there?
3. Is there a telephone in the kitchen?
4. Is there a television in the living room?
5. Is there a VCR under the television?
6. Are there a lot of books in your bedroom?
7. Are there any pictures on the wall?

T 8.7 Different rooms

There's a cat on the sofa, and there's a telephone on a small table next to the sofa. There's a CD player with some CDs under it. Not a lot of CDs. There isn't a TV, and there aren't any pictures or photographs on the walls. There's one lamp; it's next to the table with the telephone. There are two tables and two armchairs. There are some books under one of the tables.

T 8.8 Sydney

How to have a good time in ... Sydney

Sydney has everything you want in a city. It's beautiful, it has old and new buildings, there are fantastic beaches, and the food is delicious.

When to go

The best times to visit are the spring and fall. In the summer it is very hot.

Where to stay

There are cheap hotels in King's Cross. A room is about $50 a night. There are international hotels in the center. Here a room is about $150 a night.

What to do

Sydney has theaters and movie theaters, and of course, the Opera House. The best stores are on Pitt Street.

Go to the harbor. There are beaches, walks, parks, cafes, and, of course, the wonderful bridge.

Sydney has the famous Bondi Beach. People go swimming, surfing, windsurfing, and sailing.

For nightlife, there are a lot of clubs on Oxford Street.

What to eat

There are restaurants from every country—Italian, Turkish, Lebanese, Japanese, Thai, Chinese, and Vietnamese. Australians eat a lot of seafood—it's very fresh!

How to travel

There are fast trains and slow buses. The best way to see Sydney is by ferry.

T 8.9 My hometown

G'day! My name is Darren, and I live in a house with my brother and a friend. We live in Bondi and we all love surfing. We often go surfing in the morning before work.

I'm an engineer. I work in the center of Sydney for a big international company. I go to work by train. My office is on Macarthur Street, very near the Harbor. On Monday, Wednesday, and Friday I go running at lunchtime. It's very hot in the summer, but it's beautiful. I sometimes go with friends from work. We run near the Opera House.

My girlfriend likes to go shopping on Saturday. There is a great market in Paddington, and there are some great clothes shops on Oxford Street. On Saturday night, we often go to Chinatown. The food is fantastic, and really cheap. Or we stay in Bondi because there are a lot of really good little Thai and Italian restaurants here.

I usually relax on Sunday. When the weather is good, we go to the beach—Manly Beach. We go by ferry. When it's wet, we go to the movies.

T 8.10 Directions

1. Go down Main Street. Turn right at the Grand Hotel onto Charles Street. It's next to the movie theater.
2. Go straight ahead, past Charles Street and turn left onto Cherry Lane. It's on the right, next to the Italian restaurant.
3. Go down Main Street. Turn right at the bookstore. Go down River Road. It's a big building on the right.
4. Go down Main Street. Turn left at the bank onto Charles Street. It's on the right, next to the theater.
5. Go straight ahead. It's on Main Street, on the left, past the theater.

Unit 9

T 9.1 Listen and underline

1. fourteen twenty-six
2. seventeen ninety-nine
3. eighteen eighty
4. nineteen thirty-nine
5. nineteen sixty-one
6. two thousand seven

T 9.2 see p. 60

T 9.3 When were they born?

Leonardo da Vinci was a painter and scientist. He was born in 1452 in Tuscany, Italy. Marie Curie was a scientist. She was born in 1867 in Warsaw, Poland.

T 9.4 see p. 61

T 9.5 see p. 61

T 9.6 Calico Jones

My name is Calico. I know, it's a funny name! I was born in 1988. My two brothers are Henry and William, they were born … umm … Henry in 1992, and William just one year later in 1993. Ugh! They're awful! My little sister is Cleo, she's OK. She was born in 1999. Mom and Dad are Linda and Adam. My mom was born in 1961 and my dad … umm … I think he was born in 1961, too. And my grandmother … oh, she was born … uhh … in 1930 something, I think. … Yeah, in 1937. Her name's Violet. I think it's a beautiful name.

T 9.7 Listen and write

1. Shakespeare was born in England in 1564.
2. Frida Kahlo was born in Mexico in 1907.
3. Marilyn Monroe was born in the US in 1926.
4. Beethoven was born in Germany in 1770.
5. Elvis Presley was born in the US in 1935.
6. Diana Spencer was born in England in 1961.
7. Ayrton Senna was born in Brazil in 1960.
8. Indira Gandhi was born in India in 1917.

T 9.8 see p. 62

T 9.9 see p. 63

T 9.10 Listen, check and repeat

1. Ayrton Senna was an actor.
   No, he wasn't. He was a race-car driver.
2. Marie Curie was a princess.
   No, she wasn't. She was a scientist.
3. Marilyn Monroe and Elvis Presley were Mexican.
   No, they weren't. They were American.
4. Beethoven was a scientist.
   No, he wasn't. He was a musician.
5. Leonardo da Vinci and Frida Kahlo were musicians.
   No, they weren't. They were painters.
6. Indira Gandhi was a singer.
   No, she wasn't. She was a politician.

T 9.11 Past simple—irregular verbs

are	were
is	was
buy	bought
go	went
say	said
see	saw
take	took

T 9.12 We're millionaires!

In August 1999 three friends, Charles Proust, Robert Fadat, and Georges Leclerc, were on vacation in the town of Laraque in France. On Sunday they went shopping at the market and they saw a dirty, old painting. They bought it for 1,400 francs and they took it to Paris. In Paris, an expert said that the painting was by Leonardo da Vinci and it was worth 500,000,000 francs. The man at the Laraque market said: "I was happy to sell the painting, but now I'm very upset. I don't want to think about it!"

T 9.13 When's your birthday?

January
February
March
April
May
June
July
August
September
October
November
December

T 9.14 see p. 66

T 9.15 see p. 67

T 9.16 Listen and write

January first
March third
April seventh
May twentieth
June second
August twelfth
November fifteenth
December thirty-first

Unit 10

T 10.1 Listen, check and repeat

1. We're at school now.
2. You were at home yesterday.
3. I went to Australia in 1997.
4. She lives in Chicago now.
5. They bought their house in 1997.
6. It was cold and wet yesterday.

T 10.2 Becky

Yesterday was Sunday, so I got up late—eleven thirty. I had a big breakfast: orange juice, toast, eggs, and coffee. Then I went shopping, to the supermarket, and I bought some chocolate and a Sunday newspaper, the *Sunday News*. In the afternoon I listened to music a little and then I watched a movie on TV. In the evening I cooked dinner just for me—not a big meal, just soup and a salad. I went to bed early. It was a wonderful, lazy day.

T 10.3 Listen and repeat

work	worked
watch	watched
cook	cooked
play	played
stay	stayed
listen	listened

T 10.4

visit	visited
want	wanted
hate	hated

T 10.5 Becky and Dan

B = Becky   D = Dan

B Hi, Dan. Did you have a good weekend?
D Yes, I did, thanks.
B What did you do yesterday?
D Well, yesterday morning I got up early and I played tennis with some friends.
B You got up early on Sunday!
D I know, I know. I don't usually get up early on Sunday.
B Did you go out yesterday afternoon?
D No, I didn't. I just stayed home and watched basketball on TV.
B Ugh, basketball! What did you do yesterday evening?
D Oh, I didn't do much. I worked a little on my computer. I didn't go to bed late, about 11:00.

T 10.6 Listen and check

1. **B** Did you have a good weekend?
   D Yes, I did.
2. **B** What did you do yesterday?
   D I played tennis.
3. **B** Did you go out yesterday afternoon?
   D No, I didn't.
4. **B** What did you do yesterday evening?
   D I didn't do much. I didn't go to bed late.

T 10.7 Listen and repeat

Did you get up early?
Yes, I did.
Did she get up early?
No, she didn't.
We didn't go to work.
They didn't go to work.

T 10.8 Did you have a good weekend?

1. **A** I went to the movies.
   B What did you see?
2. **A** I went shopping.
   B What did you buy?
3. **A** I had dinner in a restaurant.
   B What did you have?
4. **A** I saw my friends.
   B Who did you see?
5. **A** I played soccer.
   B Where did you play?
6. **A** I went to a party.
   B What time did you leave?
7. **A** I did my homework.
   B How much homework did you do?
8. **A** I did the housework.
   B How much housework did you do?

T 10.9 see p. 71

T 10.10 Listen and check

1. Do you work in New York? No, I don't.
2. Did she like the movie? Yes, she did.
3. Does he watch TV every night? Yes, he does.
4. Did you go out last night? No, we didn't.
5. Did he go to the party? Yes, he did.
6. Do you buy a newspaper every morning? Yes, I do.
7. Does she usually go to bed late? No, she doesn't.
8. Did they have a good time? No, they didn't.

T 10.11 Vacations

B = Bill   K = Kelly

B Well, usually we go on vacation in the summer.
K Yes, and usually we go to California …, but last year we …
B … last year we went to Colorado, and we went in the winter.
K We stayed in an apartment and we cooked all our own meals there. It was wonderful.
B Yes, in California we usually stay in a hotel and eat in restaurants.
K It was good to do different things, too. Usually we just go swimming and sit in the sun …
C And I sometimes play golf. I love that!
K Ah, yes, you do. But of course in Colorado we went skiing every day, and sometimes we went ice skating in the afternoons—it was a lot of fun.
C And in the evenings we cooked dinner and then played cards. We had a very good time.
K We love vacations—we always have a good time in California, too.

T 10.12 Listen and check

1. Last year Bill and Kelly didn't go on vacation in the summer. They went in the winter.
2. They didn't go to California. They went to Colorado.
3. They didn't stay in a hotel. They stayed in an apartment.
4. They didn't eat in restaurants. They cooked their own meals.
5. They didn't go swimming. They went skiing.

Unit 11

T 11.1 What can they do?

1. Josh is a student. He can use a computer.
2. Tamika is an athlete. She can run fast.
3. Laura is an architect. She can draw well.
4. Ted is an interpreter. He can speak Chinese and Japanese.
5. John is a farmer. He can drive a tractor.
6. Helen is a grandmother. She can make cakes.

T 11.2 see p. 77

T 11.3 see p. 77

T 11.4 Josh

T = Teresa   J = Josh

T Can you use a computer, Josh?
J Yes, of course I can. All my friends can. I use a computer at school and at home.
T That's very good. What other things can you do?
J Well, I can run fast—very fast—and I can draw a little. I can draw planes and cars really well but I can't drive a car, of course. When I grow up I want to be a farmer and drive a tractor.
T And I know you can speak French.
J Yes, I can. I can speak French very well because my dad's Canadian, from Quebec. We sometimes speak French at home.
T Can you speak any other languages?
J No, I can't. I can't speak Spanish or Portuguese, just French—and English of course! And I can cook! I can make cakes. My

grandmother makes delicious cakes and I sometimes help her. Yesterday we made a big chocolate cake.

T 11.5 Pronunciation

1. I can use a computer.
2. She can't speak Thai.
3. He can speak English very well.
4. Why can't you come to my party?
5. We can't understand our teacher.
6. They can read music.
7. Can we have an ice cream?
8. Can't cats swim?

T 11.6 Tito

I come from Argentina, but now I live and work in the United States, in Los Angeles. I can speak four languages— Spanish, of course, Portuguese, Japanese, and English. I can speak English very well now, but in the beginning it was very difficult for me. I can drive a car and I can ride a horse. Back home in Argentina, I didn't drive a lot, but in Los Angeles I drive every day! I can ski, but I can't cook very well and I can't play the piano—but I can play the guitar.

T 11.7 Requests and offers

1. Can you tell me the time, please?
   It's about three thirty.
2. Can you come to my party?
   I'm sorry, I can't. It's my grandmother's birthday.
3. Can you speak more slowly, please?
   I'm sorry. Can you understand now?
4. Can I help you?
   Yes, please. I want to buy this postcard.
5. Can I have a cold drink, please?
   Yes, of course. Do you want soda or orange juice?

T 11.8 see p. 80

T 11.9 Listen to the people

Carmen
I use the Internet a lot. Every day, I think. It helps me with my homework. It helps me with everything. Yesterday I did an English test. It was quite difficult.

Anela
My brother's in Taiwan. I can't call Taiwan, it's very expensive—so Paul (that's my brother) and I—we "talk" in chat rooms on the Internet. We talk late, at about 11 o'clock in the evening—well, it's evening here, but it's 8 o'clock in the morning in Taiwan.

Tito
I play the guitar and I can find lots of songs on the Internet. Last week I got the words and music for "Can't Buy Me Love," you know, by the Beatles. I can play it now. I use the Internet on weekends because it's cheap then.

Liam
Well, my family's name is Connelly and I want to write about my family, so every day I chat with people from all over the world—Canada, South Africa, Australia—people who have the name Connelly. They send me information about their families. It's really interesting.

Tommy
I play games. And I go to chat rooms. And I visit web sites for my favorite groups and basketball

players. I want to be on the web all the time, but my mom says I can't. She says I can only use it after school for an hour, and then I stop.

April
I go shopping on the Internet. Every Friday I go to my son's house and I use his computer. It's fantastic—the supermarket brings all my food to my home!

T 11.10 What's the problem?

1. A Come on! It's time to go to the airport.
   B But I can't find my passport.
   A You put it in your bag.
   B Did I? Oh, yes. Here it is! *Phew!*
2. A Excuse me!
   B Yes?
   A This ticket machine doesn't work. I put in two dollars, but I didn't get a ticket.
   B Did you push this button?
   A Oh! No, I didn't.
   B Ah, well. There you are.
   A Thank you very much.
3. A Excuse me!
   B Yes?
   A Can you help me? I'm lost.
   B Where do you want to go?
   A To the Sherwood Hotel.
   B Go straight ahead. About 200 meters. It's on your left.
   A Thank you.
4. A I don't understand this word.
   B Check it in your dictionary.
   A My dictionary's at home. Can I borrow yours?
   B OK. No problem. Here you are.
5. A Oh, no!
   B What's the matter?
   A The TV's broken.
   B Good! Maybe we can talk this evening.
   A But I want to watch a movie.
   B Then go to the movie theater.
6. A I'm really sorry. I forgot your birthday.
   B It doesn't matter.
   A It was on the tenth, wasn't it?
   B Yes, it was.
   A Well, here are some flowers.
   B Oh, thank you. They're beautiful.

Unit 12

T 12.1 Listen and check

You can buy stamps in a post office.
You can buy a dictionary in a bookstore.
You can buy a computer magazine at a newsstand.
You can change money in a bank.
You can buy a CD in a music store.
You can get a cup of coffee in a cafe.
You can send an e-mail in an Internet cafe.

T 12.2 A trip into town

E = Enrique

1. E Good morning. I'd like a stamp for this letter to Venezuela, please.
   A That's 80¢.
   E Here you are.
   A Here's your stamp, and 20¢ change.
   E Thanks a lot. Bye.

2. E I'd like a cup of coffee, please.
   B Would you like milk and sugar?
   E No. Black, please.
   B All right. Here you are. A dollar fifty, please.
3. E Hi. I'd like to buy a Spanish/English dictionary.
   C OK. Would you like a big dictionary or a minidictionary?
   E Just a minidictionary, please.
   C This one is $6.50.
   E That's good. Thank you very much.

T 12.3 see p. 85

T 12.4 Where is Enrique?

E = Enrique

1. A Hi. Can I help you?
   E Yes. I'd like the new CD by Gary Alright, please.
   A There you are.
   E How much is that?
   A $17.99.
   E Thank you very much.
2. E I'd like to send an e-mail, please.
   B Take computer number ten.
   E Thanks a lot.
3. E Hi. I'd like this month's *PC Worldwide* magazine, please.
   C Here you are. That's $4.25, please.
   E Thank you. Bye.
4. E Two tickets for James Bond, please.
   D That's $19.50, please.
   E Thanks. What time does the movie start?
   D Seven thirty.
   E Thanks very much.
5. F Good afternoon. Can I help you?
   E Yes, please. I'd like to change some traveler's checks, please.
   F All right. Are they in American dollars?
   E Yes, they are.
   F OK. That's $150.
   E Thank you very much.

T 12.5 It's my birthday!

Suzanne
What would I like for my birthday? That's easy. I'd like to have breakfast in bed. With the newspapers. And in the evening I'd like to go to the theater.

Tom
Well, I'd like a new computer because my computer is so old that the new programs don't work on it. And then in the evening, I'd like to go to a nice restaurant. I don't care if it's Italian, Japanese, Chinese, or Indian—just good food.

Alice
I don't have a cell phone, but all my friends have one, so what I'd really like is my own cell phone. They aren't expensive these days. And in the evening, I'd like to go out with all my friends and have a great time!

T 12.6 Listening and pronunciation

1. Would you like a soda?
2. I like orange juice.
3. We'd like to go for a walk.
4. What do you like doing on the weekend?
5. We like our new car.

T 12.7 see p. 88

T 12.8 Joe's Diner

W = Waiter   P = Paul   A = Andrea

W Are you ready to order?
P Yes, we are. Andrea, what would you like to start?
A Can I have the tomato juice, please?
P And I'd like the chicken soup.
W And for your main course?
A I would like the uh, … roast chicken, please.
W OK. And for you?
P Can I have the steak, please?
W How would you like it cooked?
P Medium.
W What would you like to drink?
P Can I have a cup of coffee, please?
W Certainly.
A We'd like a bottle of mineral water, too.
W Thank you very much.
[*pause*]
W Is everything OK?
A Delicious, thank you.

T 12.9 She only eats junk food

1. When was Mary Alston's birthday?
   It was yesterday.
2. Did she have a party?
   Yes, she did.
3. Does she eat fresh food?
   No, she doesn't.
4. What does she eat?
   Popcorn, pizza, and burgers.
5. What was her job?
   She was a teacher.
6. Where was she born?
   On a farm in Pennsylvania.
7. When did she marry?
   She married in 1915.
8. What time does she get up?
   She gets up at six o'clock.
9. Where does she go every Friday?
   She goes to the hairdresser.
10. What did she say to her granddaughter?
    "I'd like a cheeseburger and fries!"

T 12.10 Going shopping

1. A Excuse me! Where can I buy film for my camera?
   B In a drugstore.
   A Is there a drugstore near here?
   B Yes, 200 meters from here, next to the bank.
2. A Can I help you?
   B No, thanks. I'm just looking.
3. A Excuse me! Do you have this shirt in a medium?
   B No, I'm sorry. That's all we have.
4. A I'd like to try on a pair of jeans, please.
   B Sure. What size are you?
   A I think I'm a 26.
   B OK. The fitting rooms are over there.
5. A Yes, miss. What would you like?
   B I'd like a kilo of potatoes, please.
   A Anything else?
   B No, that's all, thanks. How much is that?
6. A Excuse me! Do you sell Korean newspapers?
   B No, I'm sorry, we don't.
   A Where can I buy them?
   B Try the hotel.

Unit 13

T 13.1 **Listen and check**
1. George's jacket is black. Sadie's jacket is red.
2. His pants are gray. Her pants are green.
3. Her shirt is yellow. His shirt is white.
4. Her shoes are blue. His shoes are brown.

T 13.2 see p. 93

T 13.3 see p. 93

T 13.4 **Listen and check**
1. He's cooking.
2. He's driving.
3. He's taking a shower.
4. She's writing.
5. She's skiing.
6. She's eating ice cream.
7. They're running.
8. They're dancing.
9. They're playing soccer.

T 13.5 see p. 94

T 13.6 **Asking questions**
1. A What are you reading?
   B A love story.
2. A What are you watching?
   B The news.
3. A Where are you going?
   B To my bedroom.
4. A Why are you wearing three sweaters?
   B Because I'm cold.
5. A What are you eating?
   B Chocolate.
6. A How many cakes are you making?
   B Five.
7. A Who are you talking to?
   B My girlfriend.

T 13.7 see p. 98

T 13.8 **Listen and complete**
1. She has long, blonde hair.
2. He has short, black hair.
3. She has blue eyes.
4. He has brown eyes.

T 13.9 **What's the matter?**
1. She's cold.
2. He's hungry.
3. They're tired.
4. He's thirsty.
5. They're hot.
6. She's bored.

T 13.10 see p. 99

Unit 14

T 14.1 **Elena**
I'm going on vacation to Mexico next Friday, so next week's very busy. On Monday I'm picking up my tickets from the travel agent's. I'm going on vacation with my friends Grant and Nickie, so on Tuesday I'm meeting them after work and we're going shopping. On Wednesday I'm seeing the doctor at 11 o'clock, then I'm having lunch with mom. On Thursday I'm leaving work early and I'm packing. I'm taking just a bag and a backpack. Then it's Friday. Friday's the big day! At six thirty in the morning I'm going by taxi to the airport. I'm meeting Grant and Nickie there and at nine thirty we're flying to Mexico City. I'm very excited!

T 14.2 see p. 101

T 14.3 **Listen and check**
A What are you doing?
B I'm reading about Mexico.
A Why?
B Because I'm going there on vacation soon.
A Oh, how nice! When are you leaving?
B We're leaving next Friday.
A Who are you going with?
B My friends Grant and Nickie.
A How are you traveling?
B We're traveling by plane to Mexico City, then by bus and train around the country.
A Where are you staying?
B We're staying in small hotels and hostels.
A You're so lucky! Have a good time!
B Thank you very much.

T 14.4 **Marco's vacation plans**
A Marco's going on vacation.
B Oh, where's he going?
A To Banff, in Canada.
B Why is he going there?
A Because it's good for skiing and he wants to go skiing.
B When is he leaving?
A Next week—on March third.
B How is he traveling?
A By plane to Vancouver and then by car to Banff.
B Where is he staying?
A In the Banff Springs Hotel.
B And how long is he staying?
A Just ten days.

T 14.5 **Listen, check, and repeat**
1. I got up early.
   Are you getting up early tomorrow?
2. I went swimming.
   Are you going swimming tomorrow?
3. I walked to work.
   Are you walking to work tomorrow?
4. I had lunch in my office.
   Are you having lunch in your office tomorrow?

5. I left work late.
   Are you leaving work late tomorrow?
6. I met a friend.
   Are you meeting a friend tomorrow?
7. We had dinner in a restaurant.
   Are you having dinner in a restaurant tomorrow?

T 14.6 **A musical interlude**
(three music excerpts)

T 14.7 see p. 104

T 14.8 **"This Land Is Your Land"**
This land is your land, this land is my land
From California to the New York island;
From the redwood forest to the Gulf Stream waters
This land was made for you and me.

As I was walking that ribbon of highway,
I saw above me that blue, blue skyway;
I saw below me that golden valley;
This land was made for you and me.

When the sun came shining, and I was strolling,
And the wheat fields waving and the dust clouds rolling,
As the fog was lifting a voice was chanting
This land was made for you and me.

Nobody living can ever stop me,
As I go walking that freedom highway;
Nobody living can make me turn back,
This land was made for you and me.

T 14.9 **Transportation and travel**
1. We wanted to go on vacation to Rome.
2. We made a reservation for the hotel and the flight.
3. We picked up our tickets from the travel agent's.
4. We packed our bags.
5. We went to the airport.
6. We caught the plane.
7. We arrived in Rome.
8. We went sightseeing.
9. We had a great time.

T 14.10 **Going sightseeing**
1. A Hi. Can I help you?
   B Yes. I'd like a map of the city, please.
   A Here you are.
   B Thank you.
2. C We'd like to go on a bus tour of the city.
   A OK. The next bus leaves at ten. It takes an hour.
   C Where does the bus leave from?
   A It leaves from the bus station on Maple Street.
3. D We'd like to visit the museum. When is it open?
   A From nine o'clock to five o'clock every day.
   D How much is it to get in?
   A Ten dollars for adults and it's free for children.

Grammar Reference

Unit 1

1.1 *am/are/is*

I	'm am	John Clark. fine.
You	're are	Kazu.
My name	's is	Sandra.
This	is	

1.2 Questions with question words

What's your name?   *what's = what is*
How are you?

1.3 Possessive adjectives

My name's John.
What's **your** name?

1.4 Plural nouns

1. Most nouns add *-s.*
book	book**s**
computer	computer**s**
camera	camera**s**

2. Some nouns add *-es.*
sandwich	sandwich**es**

Unit 2

2.1 *am/are/is*

I	'm (am)	
You	're (are)	fine. a student. from Japan.
He She	's (is)	

2.2 Possessive adjectives

His name's Fu-an.
What's **her** name?

My name's Maria.
What's **your** name?

🔔 *his* = possessive adjective
his name, his car, his camera

he's = he is
He's Miguel. He's from Brazil. He's fine.

2.3 Questions with question words

Where	are you is she is he	from?
What	's your (is your) 's her (is her)	name?

2.4 *am/are/is*

I	'm (am)	
You	're (are)	from Canada. a student. fine. in Tokyo. in New York. married.
He She It	's (is)	
They	're (are)	

Unit 3

3.1 *am/is*

Negative

I	'm not (am not)	a teacher. from Taiwan. married. OK.
He She	isn't (is not)	

Yes/No questions and short answers

Are you married?	Yes, I am. No, I'm not.
Is she a teacher?	Yes, she is. No, she isn't.
Is he American?	Yes, he is. No, he isn't.
Is her name Alicia?	Yes, it is. No, it isn't.

3.2 *am/are/is* (verb *to be*)

Affirmative

I	'm (am)	
He She It	's (is)	from the US.
You We They	're (are)	

Negative

I	'm not	
He She It	isn't	American.
You We They	aren't	

Questions with question words

What	is your name? is her address? is his phone number?
Where	are you from? is he from? are they from?
How old	are you? are they?

Answers

John Clark.
16 Main Street, Dallas.
(972) 555-6729.

From Mexico.

I'm 16.
They're 8 and 10.

Yes/No questions

Is	he she it	English?
Are	you we they	married?

Short answers

Yes, he is.
No, she isn't.
Yes, it is.

Yes, I am.
No, we aren't.
No, they aren't.

Unit 4

4.1 Possessive adjectives

This is	my your his her our their	book.

4.2 Possessive 's

's shows possession.

my son	→	John's son
your job	→	Patty's job
his house	→	Tom's house
her name	→	your wife's name

🛈 *'s* is also the short form of *is*.

he's	=	he is
she's	=	she is
it's	=	it is
Who's	=	Who is

4.3 Plural nouns

1. Most nouns add *-s* in the plural.

doctor	→	doctors
book	→	books
student	→	students

2. Nouns that end in *-s*, *-ss*, *-sh*, or *ch* add *-es*.

bus	→	buses
class	→	classes
sandwich	→	sandwiches

3. Some nouns that end in *-y* change to *-ies*.

city	→	cities
country	→	countries
dictionary	→	dictionaries

4. Some nouns are irregular.

man	→	men
woman	→	women
child	→	children

4.4 *have/has*

Have is an irregular verb.

I You We They	have	a good job. a computer.
He She It	has	

Unit 5

5.1 Present Simple—*I / you / we / they*

Affirmative

I You We They	like coffee. play tennis. live in Denver. speak two languages. have a good job.

Negative

I You We They	don't	like tennis. speak Spanish. work in a restaurant.

Questions with question words

Where		you live?
What sports	do	we like?
How many languages		they speak?

Yes/No questions and short answers

Do you like basketball?	Yes, I do. No, I don't.
Do they speak English?	Yes, they do. No, they don't.

🛈 Do you like tea? Yes, I do. NOT ~~Yes, I like.~~

5.2 *a/an*

We use *an* before words that begin with *a, e, i, o,* and *u.*

an actor
an English dictionary
an ice cream
an orange
an umbrella

but

a car
a hamburger
a television

5.3 adjective + noun

Adjectives always come *before* the noun.

an **American** car		~~a car American~~
a **Japanese** camera	NOT	~~a camera Japanese~~
a **beautiful** girl		~~a girl beautiful~~

🛈 Spanish oranges NOT ~~Spanishes oranges~~

Unit 6

6.1 Present Simple *he / she / it*

Affirmative

He She	gets up	at 8:00.
It	leaves	

6.2 Spelling – Present Simple *he / she / it*

1. Most verbs add -*s*.
   - he   listen**s**
   - she   leave**s**
   - it   walk**s**

2. Verbs ending in -*s*, -*ss*, -*sh*, -*ch* add -*es*.
   - he
   - she   watch**es**
   - it   wash**es**

   ❗ *go*, *have*, and *do* are irregular.
   - he   does
   - she   goes
   - it   has

6.3 Adverbs of frequency

0%	40%	90%
never	sometimes	usually

These adverbs usually come before the verb.
We **never** go out in the evening.
He **usually** goes to work by taxi.
She **sometimes** has a cup of coffee.

6.4 Present Simple *he / she / it*

Negative

She He	doesn't	go out in the evening. eat in a restaurant.

Questions with question words

What Where When	does	he do in the evening? she have lunch?
		it leave?

Yes/No questions and short answers

Does he like basketball?	Yes, he does. No, he doesn't.
Does she speak English?	Yes, she does. No, she doesn't.

❗ Does he like tea?   Yes, he does.   NOT   ~~Yes, he likes.~~

Unit 7

7.1 Question words

Look at the question words and the answers.

What?	A hamburger.
When?	In the evening.
What time?	At 8:00.
Who?	Peter.
Where?	In Bangkok.
How?	By taxi.
How old?	16.
How many?	Two.
How much?	$2.
Why?	Because …

7.2 Object pronouns

Look at the subject and object pronouns, and the possessive adjectives.

Subject pronouns	Object pronouns	Possessive adjectives
I	me	my
you	you	your
he	him	his
she	her	her
it	it	its
we	us	our
they	them	their

7.3 *this/that*

We use *this* to refer to things near to us.

This is my son.   I like this sandwich.

We use *that* to refer to things that are not near to us.

That's my dog.   I don't like that car.

Unit 8

8.1 *There is/There are*

Affirmative
There's a sofa in the living room. (*There's = There is*)
There are two CD players in my house.

Question
Is there a TV in the kitchen?
Are there any magazines on the table?
How many CDs **are there**?

Negative
There isn't a TV.
There aren't any photos.

8.2 *any*

We use *any* in questions and negatives.
Are there any books in the room?
There are**n't any** CDs.

Unit 9

9.1 *was/were*

Was and *were* are the past tense of *am/are/is*.

Present affirmative
I **am** happy.
You **are** a student.
He/She/It **is** in London.
We **are** hot.
They **are** at work.

Past affirmative
I **was** happy yesterday.
You **were** a student in 1998.
He/She/It **was** in London.
We **were** hot.
They **were** at work last week.

Negative

| I
He | wasn't | home last weekend.
at school yesterday. |
| You
They | weren't | |

Questions
Where **were you** yesterday?
Was she at school? Yes, **she was.**/No, **she wasn't.**

❶ We use *was/were* with *born*, not *am/is/are*.
Where were you born?
He was born in Korea.   NOT   Where ~~are~~ you born?
He ~~is~~ born in Korea.

9.2 Past Simple—irregular verbs

Many common verbs are irregular. See the list of irregular verbs on p. 142.

Present	Past
is/are	was/were
buy	bought
go	went
say	said
see	saw
take	took

Unit 10

10.1 Past Simple affirmative

1. Regular verbs add *-ed* or *-d* in the Past Simple.

Present	Past
play	play**ed**
watch	watch**ed**
listen	listen**ed**
turn	turn**ed**
change	chang**ed**

2. Many common verbs are irregular.
go   went
see   saw
have   had
See the list on p. 142.

3. The form is the same for all persons.

I You He/She/It We They	listened to music. went to work. had lunch.

10.2 Past Simple questions and negatives

❶ Present *do/does* → Past *did*
What time **does** he usually get up?
What time **did** he get up yesterday?

Questions with question words

Where	did	I you he/she/it we they	go?

Negative

I We	didn't	go shopping. see my friends.

Yes/No questions and short answers

Did they play soccer?	Yes, they did.
Did you have a good time?	No, I didn't.

Unit 11

11.1 *can*

Affirmative

I You He/She/It We They	can	swim. drive. cook. run fast.

Negative

I You He/She/It We They	can't	draw. speak Chinese. play golf.

Questions with question words

When		I go home?
What	can	you do?
How many languages		he speak?

Yes/No questions and short answers

Can you swim?	Yes, I can.
Can he play tennis?	No, he can't.

Unit 12

12.1 *would like*

1. We use *would like* to ask for things.
   I'd like a magazine, please.   'd = would
   We'd like a cup of coffee, please.

2. We use *would like* in questions to offer things.
   Would you **like** some cake?   Yes, please.
   Would you **like** a drink?   No, thank you.

   ⓘ Would you like a cup of coffee?
   No, thank you.   NOT ~~No, I wouldn't.~~

3. We can use *would like* with another verb.
   Would you like **to go out** tonight?
   What would you like **to do**?

12.2 *like* and *would like*

1. We use *like* and *like doing* to talk about things we always like.
   I **like** coffee. (= I always enjoy coffee.)
   She **likes** swimming in the summer.
   What do you **like** doing on the weekend?

2. We use *would like* to talk about things we want *now*.
   I'd like a cup of coffee. (= I want a cup of coffee now.)
   She's hot. She**'d like** to go swimming.
   What **would** you **like** to do tonight?

12.3 *would like* and *want*

We use *would like*, not *want*, when we want to be polite.
   I'd like a cup of tea, please.   NOT ~~I want a cup of tea.~~
   Would you like an ice cream?

Unit 13

13.1 Present Continuous

Affirmative

I	am	
He She It	is	working.
You We They	are	

13.2 Present Continuous

Negative

I	'm not	
He She It	isn't	working.
You We They	aren't	

Questions with question words

	am I	
What	are you are we are they	wearing?
	is he is she	

Yes/No questions and short answers

Are you wearing jeans?	Yes, I am. No, I'm not.
Is she reading a newspaper?	Yes, she is. No, she isn't.

13.3 Present Simple and Present Continuous

1. We use the Present Simple to talk about actions that are true for all time or a long time.
   Jun **comes** from Korea.
   I **love** you.
   My father **works** in a bank.
   I **get up** at 7:30 every day.
   She **doesn't understand** Portuguese.

2. We use the Present Continuous to talk about actions that last a short time. The actions are happening *now*.
   I usually wear jeans, but today I**'m wearing** a suit.
   He**'s speaking** Thai to that man. He speaks Thai very well.
   It**'s raining**.
   They**'re swimming**.

Unit 14

14.1 Present Continuous for future

1. See **Grammar Reference 13.1** and **13.2** for the forms of the Present Continuous—affirmative, negative, questions, and short answers.

2. We also use the Present Continuous to express **future plans**.
   We're flying to Mexico **on Friday**.
   I'm having lunch with Mary **on Tuesday**.
   What are you doing **this weekend**?
   I'm seeing the doctor **this week**.
   We're having a party **next Saturday**. Can you come?

Word List

Here is a list of most of the new words in the units of *American Headway Starter*.

adj = adjective
adv = adverb
conj = conjunction
n = noun
pl = plural
prep = preposition
pron = pronoun
v = verb
infml = informal

Unit 1

and *conj* /ænd/, /ənd/
bag *n* /bæg/
book *n* /bʊk/
camera *n* /'kæmrə/
car *n* /kɑr/
computer *n* /kəm'pyutər/
fine *adj* /faɪn/
good *adj* /gʊd/
hamburger *n* /'hæmbərgər/
hello /hɛ'loʊ/
hi /haɪ/
house *n* /haʊs/
How are you? /ˌhaʊ ər 'yu/
it *pron* /ɪt/
my *adj* /maɪ/
name *n* /neɪm/
number *n* /'nʌmbər/
OK /ˌoʊ'keɪ/
photograph *n* /'foʊtəgræf/
sandwich *n* /'sænwɪtʃ/
student *n* /'studənt/
television *n* /'tɛləvɪʒn/
thanks *infml* /θæŋks/
this *pron* /ðɪs/
what? /wʌt/
your *adj* /yər/

Numbers 1–10
one /wʌn/
two /tu/
three /θri/
four /fɔr/
five /faɪv/
six /sɪks/
seven /'sɛvən/
eight /eɪt/
nine /naɪn/
ten /tɛn/

Unit 2

Australia *n* /ɔ'streɪlyə/
Brazil *n* /brə'zɪl/
Canada *n* /'kænədə/
center *n* /'sɛntər/
city *n* /'sɪti/
country *n* /'kʌntri/
doctor *n* /'dɑktər/
England *n* /'ɪŋglənd/
from *prep* /frʌm/, /frəm/
her *adj* /hər/
his *adj* /hɪz/
hospital *n* /'hɑspɪtl/
in *prep* /ɪn/
it *pron* /ɪt/
Japan *n* /dʒə'pæn/
Korea *n* /kə'riə/
married *adj* /'mærid/
Mexico *n* /'mɛksɪkoʊ/
school *n* /skul/
Taiwan *n* /taɪ'wɑn/
teacher *n* /'titʃər/
the United States *n* /ðə yu,naɪtəd 'steɪts/
too *adv* /tu/
where *adv* /wɛr/
world *n* /wərld/

Numbers 11–30
eleven /ɪ'lɛvən/
twelve /twɛlv/
thirteen /ˌθər'tin/
fourteen /ˌfɔr'tin/
fifteen /ˌfɪf'tin/
sixteen /ˌsɪk'stin/
seventeen /ˌsɛvən'tin/
eighteen /ˌeɪ'tin/
nineteen /ˌnaɪn'tin/
twenty /'twɛnti/, /'twʌnti/
twenty-one /ˌtwʌnti'wʌn/
twenty-two /ˌtwʌnti'tu/
twenty-three /ˌtwʌnti'θri/
twenty-four /ˌtwʌnti'fɔr/
twenty-five /ˌtwʌnti'faɪv/
twenty-six /ˌtwʌnti'sɪks/
twenty-seven /ˌtwʌnti'sɛvən/
twenty-eight /ˌtwʌnti'eɪt/
twenty-nine /ˌtwʌnti'naɪn/
thirty /'θərti/

Unit 3

address *n* /'ædrɛs/
afternoon *n* /ˌæftər'nun/
age *n* /eɪdʒ/
at *prep* /æt/
businessman *n* /'bɪznəsmæn/
dictionary *n* /'dɪkʃəˌnɛri/
Excuse me? /ɪk'skyuz mi/
good *adj* /gʊd/
good-bye /ˌgʊd'baɪ/
great (= very good) *adj* /greɪt/
have a good trip /hæv ə gʊd trɪp/
homework *n* /'hoʊmwərk/
hotel *n* /hoʊ'tɛl/
how old? *adv* /ˌhaʊ 'oʊld/
I don't know /aɪ ˌdont 'noʊ/
I don't understand /aɪ ˌdont əndər'stænd/
job *n* /dʒɑb/
morning *n* /'mɔrnɪŋ/
night *n* /naɪt/
not *adv* /nɑt/
nurse *n* /nərs/
of *prep* /ʌv/, /əv/
on tour /ˌɑn 'tʊr/
page *n* /peɪdʒ/
personal information *n* /ˌpərsənəl ɪnfər'meɪʃn/
phone number *n* /'foʊn ˌnʌmbər/
police officer *n* /pə'lis ˌɔfəsər/
pop group *n* /'pɑp grup/
sales assistant *n* /'seɪlz əˌsɪstənt/
sir *n* /sər/
sorry /'sɑri/
street *n* /strit/
taxi driver *n* /'tæksi ˌdraɪvər/
thank you /'θæŋk yu/
that's right /ðæts 'raɪt/
trip *n* /trɪp/
Venezuela *n* /ˌvɛnə'zweɪlə/
who? /hu/
workbook *n* /'wərkbʊk/

Unit 4

a lot of *adv* /ə ˈlɑt əv/
alphabet *n* /ˈælfəˌbɛt/
also *adv* /ˈɔlsoʊ/
apartment *n* /əˈpɑrtmənt/

bank *n* /bæŋk/
bank manager *n* /ˈbæŋk ˌmænədʒər/
beautiful *adj* /ˈbyutəfl/
best *adj* /bɛst/
big *adj* /bɪg/
both /boʊθ/
brother *n* /ˈbrʌðər/
bus *n* /bʌs/
business card *n* /ˈbɪznəs ˌkɑrd/
but *conj* /bʌt/, /bət/

call *v* /kɔl/
Canadian *adj* /kəˈneɪdiən/
CD *n* /ˌsiˈdi/
certainly *adv* /ˈsərtənli/
child *n* /tʃaɪld/
children *n* /ˈtʃɪldrən/
class *n* /klæs/
classroom *n* /ˈklæsrum/
college *n* /ˈkɑlɪdʒ/
company *n* /ˈkʌmpəni/
country (= not the city) *n* /ˈkʌntri/

dad *n* /dæd/
daughter *n* /ˈdɔtər/
director *n* /dəˈrɛktər/
dog *n* /dɔg/

e-mail *n* /ˈimeɪl/
evening *n* /ˈivnɪŋ/

family *n* /ˈfæmli/
fan *n* /fæn/
farm *n* /fɑrm/
father *n* /ˈfɑðər/
favorite *adj* /ˈfeɪvrɪt/
fax *n* /fæks/
first name /ˌfərst ˈneɪm/
friend *n* /frɛnd/
funny *adj* /ˈfʌni/

girlfriend *n* /ˈgərlfrɛnd/
group *n* /grʊp/

happy *adj* /ˈhæpi/
have *v* /hæv/
have a good time /ˌhæv ə gʊd ˈtaɪm/
high school *n* /ˈhaɪ ˌskul/
house *n* /haʊs/
how? *adv* /haʊ/
husband *n* /ˈhʌsbənd/

last name *n* /ˌlæst ˈneɪm/

manager *n* /ˈmænədʒər/
mother *n* /ˈmʌðər/
mom *n* /mɑm/
music *n* /ˈmyuzɪk/

near *prep* /nɪr/
nice *adj* /naɪs/

office *n* /ˈɔfəs/
our *adj* /ˈaʊər/

parent *n* /ˈpɛrənt/
part-time *adj* /ˌpɑrt ˈtaɪm/
please /pliz/

really *adv* /ˈrili/
relation *n* /rɪˈleɪʃn/
rock 'n roll *n* /ˌrɑkənˈroʊl/

sister *n* /ˈsɪstər/
small *adj* /smɔl/
son *n* /sʌn/
spell *v* /spɛl/
sport *n* /spɔrt/

their *adj* /ðɛr/
together *adv* /təˈgɛðər/
town *n* /taʊn/

Vermont *n* /vərˈmɑnt/
very *adv* /ˈvɛri/

when *adv* /wɛn/
who's calling? /ˌhuz ˈkɔlɪŋ/
wife *n* /waɪf/

Unit 5

a little *adj* /ə ˈlɪtl/
actor *n* /ˈæktər/
American *adj* /əˈmɛrɪkən/

bar of chocolate *n* /bɑr əv ˈtʃɔklət/
baseball *n* /ˈbeɪsbɔl/
basketball *n* /ˈbæskətbɔl/
be *v* /bi/
Brazilian *adj* /brəˈzɪlyən/

cell phone *n* /ˈsɛl foʊn/
cent *n* /sɛnt/
chicken *n* /ˈtʃɪkən/
China *n* /ˈtʃaɪnə/
Chinese *adj* /tʃaɪˈniz/
Cleveland *n* /ˈklivlənd/
coffee *n* /ˈkɔfi/

dollar *n* /ˈdɑlər/
downtown *adj* /ˌdaʊnˈtaʊn/
drama student *n* /ˈdrɑmə ˌstudənt/
drink *v, n* /drɪŋk/

eat *v* /it/
English *n, adj* /ˈɪŋglɪʃ/

food *n* /fud/
France *n* /fræns/
French *adj* /frɛntʃ/

German *adj* /ˈdʒərmən/

hotel *n* /hoʊˈtɛl/
how many? /haʊ ˈmɛni/
how much? *adv* /haʊ ˈmʌtʃ/

ice cream *n* /ˈaɪskrim/
identity *n* /aɪˈdɛntəti/
Italian *adj* /ɪˈtælyən/
Italy *n* /ˈɪtəli/

Japanese *adj* /ˌdʒæpəˈniz/
juice *n* /dʒus/

Korean *adj* /kəˈriən/

language *n* /ˈlæŋgwɪdʒ/
life *n* /laɪf/
like *v* /laɪk/
live *v* /lɪv/
love *v* /lʌv/

Mexican *adj* /ˈmɛksɪkən/

nationality *n* /ˌnæʃəˈnælɪti/
New York *n* /ˌnu ˈyork/
now *adv* /naʊ/

Ohio *n* /oʊˈhaɪoʊ/
orange *n* /ˈɔrɪndʒ/

party *n* /ˈpɑrti/
people *n pl* /ˈpipl/
pizza *n* /ˈpitsə/
play *v* /pleɪ/
Portuguese *adj* /ˌpɔrtʃəˈgiz/
price *n* /praɪs/

really? /ˈrili/
restaurant *n* /ˈrɛstrɑnt/

skiing *n* /ˈskiɪŋ/
soda *n* /ˈsoʊdə/
Spain *n* /speɪn/
Spanish *adj* /ˈspænɪʃ/

speak *v* /spik/
sport *n* /spɔrt/
swimming *n* /ˈswɪmɪŋ/

tea *n* /ti/
tennis *n* /ˈtɛnəs/
think *v* /θɪŋk/

waiter *n* /ˈweɪtər/
want *v* /wɑnt/
water *n* /ˈwɔtər/
work *v* /wərk/

Numbers 40–100
forty /ˈfɔrti/
fifty /ˈfɪfti/
sixty /ˈsɪksti/
seventy /ˈsɛvənti/
eighty /ˈeɪti/
ninety /ˈnaɪnti/
one hundred /wən ˈhʌndrəd/

Unit 6

after *adv* /'æftər/
artist *n* /'ɑrtɪst/
at home *adv* /æt 'hoʊm/

bed *n* /bɛd/
breakfast *n* /'brɛkfəst/
buy *v* /baɪ/
by bus /,baɪ 'bʌs/
by taxi /,baɪ 'tæksi/

clock *n* /klɑk/
cook *v* /kʊk/
cup *n* /kʌp/

day *n* /deɪ/
different *adj* /'dɪfrənt/
dinner *n* /'dɪnər/
director *n* /də'rɛktər/,
    /'daɪ,rɛktər/

early *adj* /'ərli/
evening *n* /'ivnɪŋ/
every /'ɛvri/

get home /,gɛt 'hoʊm/
get up *v* /,gɛt 'ʌp/
go *v* /goʊ/
go for a walk /,goʊ fər ə 'wɔk/
go out *v* /,goʊ 'aʊt/
go shopping /,goʊ 'ʃɑpɪŋ/
grandfather *n* /'græn,fɑðər/

have breakfast /,hæv 'brɛkfəst/
have lunch /,hæv lʌntʃ/
home *n* /hoʊm/

the Internet *n* /ðə 'ɪntərnɛt/

late *adj* /leɪt/
leave school/home /,liv 'skul,
    'hoʊm/
lifestyle *n* /'laɪfstaɪl/
listen to music /,lɪsən tə 'myuzɪk/
lunch *n* /lʌntʃ/

millionaire *n* /,mɪlyə'nɛr/

never *adv* /'nɛvər/
nine o'clock *n* /,naɪn ə'klɑk/

paint *v* /peɪnt/
play the piano /,pleɪ ðə pi'ænoʊ/

site *n* /saɪt/
soda *n* /'soʊdə/
sometimes *adv* /'sʌmtaɪmz/
stay home /,steɪ 'hoʊm/
studio *n* /'studioʊ/

take a shower /,teɪk ə 'ʃaʊər/
taxi *n* /'tæksi/
time *n* /taɪm/
toast *n* /toʊst/
today *n* /tə'deɪ/
tomorrow *n* /tə'mɑroʊ/
TV *n* /,ti'vi/

until *adv* /ən'tɪl/
usually *adv* /'yuʒuəli/

walk *v, n* /wɔk/
watch *v* /wɑtʃ/
week *n* /wik/
weekday *n* /'wikdeɪ/
weekend *n* /'wikɛnd/
what time is it? /wət 'taɪm ɪz ɪt/

when? *adv* /wɛn/
with *prep* /wɪθ, wɪð/
work *n* /wərk/

Days of the week
Monday *n* /'mʌndeɪ/
Tuesday *n* /'tuzdeɪ/
Wednesday *n* /'wɛnzdeɪ/
Thursday *n* /'θərzdeɪ/
Friday *n* /'fraɪdeɪ/
Saturday *n* /'sætərdeɪ/
Sunday *n* /'sʌndeɪ/

Unit 7

about *adv* /ə'baʊt/
activity *n* /æk'tɪvəti/
all /ɔl/
awful *adj* /'ɔfl/

beach *n* /bitʃ/
because *conj* /bɪ'kɔz, bɪ'kʌz/
boyfriend *n* /'bɔɪfrɛnd/
building *n* /'bɪldɪŋ/

cafe *n* /kæ'feɪ/
Canberra *n* /'kænbɛrə/
capital city *n* /,kæpətl 'sɪti/
cat *n* /kæt/
change a traveler's check /,tʃeɪndʒ
    ə ,trævlərz 'tʃɛk/
cheap *adj* /tʃip/
clothing store *n* /'kloʊðɪŋ ,stɔr/
cold *adj* /koʊld/
comfortable *adj* /'kʌmftərbl/

delicious *adj* /dɪ'lɪʃəs/

e-mail *n* /'imeɪl/
end *n* /ɛnd/
every /'ɛvri/
expensive *adj* /ɪk'spɛnsɪv/

famous *adj* /'feɪməs/
fantastic *adj* /fæn'tæstɪk/
first *adj* /fərst/
fitting room *n* /'fɪtɪŋ ,rum/
floor *n* /flɔr/
friendly *adj* /'frɛndli/

give *v* /gɪv/
glass *n* /glæs/

hate *v* /heɪt/
Hawaii *n* /hə'wɑii/
help *v* /hɛlp/
here *adv* /hɪr/
him *pron* /hɪm/
homework *n* /'hoʊmwərk/
hot *adj* /hɑt/

international *adj* /,ɪntər'næʃənl/
Internet cafe *n* /'ɪntərnɛt kæ,feɪ/
I see /,aɪ 'si/

jacket *n* /'dʒækət/
journalist *n* /'dʒərnlɪst/
just *adv* /dʒʌst/

marry *v* /'mæri/
math *n* /mæθ/
me *pron* /mi/
money *n* /'mʌni/
movies *n pl* /'muviz/
movie star *n* /'muvi ,star/

new *adj* /nu/

of course /,əv 'kɔrs/
old *adj* /oʊld/
one-way ticket *n* /wən,weɪ 'tɪkət/

pay *v* /peɪ/
phone *n* /foʊn/
place *n* /pleɪs/
postcard *n* /'poʊstkɑrd/
present (for someone's birthday)
    n /'prɛznt/
president *n* /'prɛzədənt/
pyramid *n* /'pɪrəmɪd/

queen *n* /kwin/
round-trip ticket *n* /raʊnd,trɪp
    'tɪkət/

see you soon /si yə 'sun/
send *v* /sɛnd/
soccer *n* /'sɑkər/
start *v* /stɑrt/
sweater *n* /'swɛtər/

teach *v* /titʃ/
that *pron* /ðæt/
them *pron* /ðɛm/
train station *n* /'treɪn ,steɪʃn/
try on (a sweater) /'traɪ ɑn/
T-shirt *n* /'tiʃərt/
tuna *n* /'tunə/

us *pron* /ʌs/

vacation *n* /veɪ'keɪʃn/
very much /vɛri mətʃ/
visit *v* /'vɪzət/

weather *n* /'wɛðər/
wedding *n* /'wɛdɪŋ/
wet *adj* /wɛt/
White House *n* /'waɪt haʊs/
why? *adv* /waɪ/
wonderful *adj* /'wʌndərfl/

you know /'yu noʊ/

Unit 8

armchair *n* /'armtʃɛr/
Australian *n* /ɔ'streɪlyən/
bathroom *n* /'bæθrum/
before *prep* /prep/
bed *n* /bɛd/
bedroom *n* /'bɛdrum/
bookstore *n* /'bʊkstɔr/
bridge *n* /brɪdʒ/
CD player *n* /si'di ,pleɪər/
chair *n* /tʃɛr/
clothes *n pl* /kloʊz/
club *n* /klʌb/
company *n* /'kʌmpəni/
credit card *n* /'krɛdət kard/
dining room *n* /'daɪnɪŋ ,rum/
drawer *n* /drɔr/
drugstore *n* /'drʌgstɔr/
engineer *n* /,ɛndʒə'nɪr/
everything *pron* /'ɛvriθɪŋ/
fall (autumn) *n* /fɔl/
far *adv* /far/
fast *adv* /fæst/
ferry *n* /'fɛri/
floor *n* /flɔr/
fresh *adj* /frɛʃ/
go running /goʊ 'rʌnɪŋ/
go straight ahead /goʊ 'streɪt ə,hɛd/
harbor *n* /'harbər/
hometown *n* /,hoʊm'taʊn/
key *n* /ki/
kitchen *n* /'kɪtʃən/
lamp *n* /læmp/
Lebanese *adj* /,lɛbə'niz/
living room *n* /'lɪvɪŋ rum/
magazine *n* /,mægə'zin/
market *n* /'markət/
movie theater *n* /'muvi ,θiətər/
near *prep* /nɪr/
newsstand *n* /'nuzstænd/
next to *prep* /nɛkstu/
nightlife *n* /'naɪtlaɪf/
often *adv* /'ɔfn/
on *prep* /an/
opera *n* /'aprə/
park *n* /park/
pen *n* /pɛn/
picture *n* /'pɪktʃər/
post office *n* /'poʊst ,ɔfəs/
room *n* /rum/
run *v* /rʌn/
sailing *n* /'seɪlɪŋ/
seafood *n* /'sifud/
shoe *n* /ʃu/
shower *n* /'ʃaʊər/
sign *n* /saɪn/
slow *adj* /sloʊ/
sofa *n* /'soʊfə/
spring *n* /sprɪŋ/
stay *v* /steɪ/
store *n* /stoʊr/

stove *n* /stoʊv/
summer *n* /'sʌmər/
supermarket *n* /'supərmarkət/
surfing *n* /'sərfɪŋ/
table *n* /'teɪbl/
Thai *adj* /taɪ/
theater *n* /'θiətər/
toilet *n* /'tɔɪlət/
train *n* /treɪn/
travel *v* /'trævl/
Turkish *adj* /'tərkɪʃ/
turn left/right /tərn lɛft, raɪt/
under *prep* /'ʌndər/
VCR *n* /,vi si 'ar/
Vietnamese *adj* /,viətnə'miz/
walk *n* /wɔk/
wall *n* /wɔl/
way (to see Sydney) *n* /weɪ/
window *n* /'wɪndoʊ/
windsurfing *n* /'wɪndsərfɪŋ/
yard *n* /yard/

Unit 9

birthday *n* /'bərθdeɪ/
calendar *n* /'kæləndər/
designer *n* /dɪ'zaɪnər/
dirty *adj* /'dərti/
expert *n* /'ɛkspərt/
for sale /fɔr 'seɪl/
India *n* /'ɪndiə/
know *v* /noʊ/
last (year) /læst/
man *n* /mæn/
market *n* /'markət/
million *n* /'mɪlyən/
month *n* /mʌnθ/
musician *n* /myu'zɪʃn/
painter *n* /'peɪntər/
painting *n* /'peɪntɪŋ/
Poland *n* /'poʊlənd/
politician *n* /,palə'tɪʃn/
princess *n* /'prɪnsɛs/
race-car driver *n* /,reɪskar 'draɪvər/
say *v* /seɪ/
scientist *n* /'saɪəntɪst/
see *v* /si/
sell *v* /sɛl/
singer *n* /'sɪŋər/
so *adv* /soʊ/
story *n* /'stɔri/

take *v* /teɪk/
tell *v* /tɛl/
think *v* /θɪŋk/
thousand /'θaʊznd/

upset *adj* /,ʌp'sɛt/
was/were born /,wəz, wər 'bɔrn/
which? /wɪtʃ/
worth *adj* /wərθ/
writer *n* /'raɪtər/
year *n* /yɪr/
yesterday *adv* /'yɛstərdeɪ/

Months of the year

January /'dʒænyuɛri/
February /'fɛbyu,ɛri/
March /martʃ/
April /'eɪprəl/
May /meɪ/
June /dʒun/
July /dʒʊ'laɪ/
August /'ɔgəst/
September /sɛp'tɛmbər/
October /ak'toʊbər/
November /noʊ'vɛmbər/
December /dɪ'sɛmbər/

Unit 10

a little /ə lɪtl/
application form *n* /,æplə'keɪʃn fɔrm/
baseball *n* /'beɪsbɔl/
cards *n pl* /kardz/
date *n* /deɪt/
date of birth *n* /deɪt əv ,bərθ/
egg *n* /ɛg/
fill in *v* /fɪl ɪn/
fitness training *n* /'fɪtnəs ,treɪnɪŋ/
form *n* /fɔrm/
fries *n pl* /fraɪz/
full name *n* /,fʊl 'neɪm/
fun *n* /fʌn/
go dancing /goʊ 'dænsɪŋ/
golf *n* /galf/
have a good weekend /hæv ə gʊd 'wikɛnd/
housework *n* /'haʊswərk/
ice hockey *n* /'aɪs ,haki/
ice skating *n* /'aɪs ,skeɪtɪŋ/
interested in /'ɪntrəstəd ɪn/
join *v* /dʒɔɪn/
lazy *adj* /'leɪzi/
leisure *n* /'liʒər/
the movies *n pl* /ðə 'muviz/
newspaper *n* /'nuzpeɪpər/
night *n* /naɪt/
orange juice *n* /'ɔrɪndʒ dʒʊs/
own *adj* /oʊn/
party *n* /'parti/
running *n* /'rʌnɪŋ/
salad *n* /'sæləd/
season *n* /'sizn/
shopping *n* /'ʃapɪŋ/
signature *n* /'sɪgnətʃər/
sit *v* /sɪt/
soup *n* /sup/
sports center *n* /'spɔrts ,sɛntər/
squash *n* /skwaʃ/
steak *n* /steɪk/
sun *n* /sʌn/
walking *n* /'wɔkɪŋ/
winter *n* /'wɪntər/
yesterday afternoon /,yɛstərdeɪ æftər'nun/
yesterday evening /,yɛstərdeɪ 'ɪvnɪŋ/
yesterday morning /,yɛstərdeɪ 'mɔrnɪŋ/
zip code *n* /'zɪp koʊd/

Unit 11

about *prep* /ə'baʊt/
airport *n* /'ɛrpɔrt/
all /ɔl/
all over the world /ˌɔl ˌoʊvər ðə 'wɜrld/
architect *n* /'arkətɛkt/
athlete *n* /'æθlit/

borrow *v* /'baroʊ/
bring *v* /brɪŋ/
broken *adj* /'broʊkn/
button *n* /'bʌtn/

cake *n* /keɪk/
can *v* /kæn, kən/
chat *v* /tʃæt/
check *v* /tʃɛk/
chess *n* /tʃɛs/
cold drink *n* /ˌkoʊld 'drɪŋk/
come *v* /cʌm/
communicate *v* /kə'myunəkeɪt/
company *n* /'kʌmpəni/
computer games *n pl* /kəm'pyutər ˌgeɪmz/

department of defense /dɪˌpartmənt əv dɪ'fɛns/
draw *v* /drɔ/
drive *v* /draɪv/

endless *adj* /'ɛndləs/

farmer *n* /'farmər/
find *v* /faɪnd/
flower *n* /'flaʊər/
forecast *n* /'fɔrkæst/
forget *v* /fər'gɛt/

grow up *v* /'groʊ əp/
guitar *n* /gɪ'tar/

hard *adj* /hard/
horse *n* /hɔrs/

the Net (Internet) *n* /ðə 'nɛt/
interpreter *n* /ɪn'tərprɛtər/
it doesn't matter /ɪt ˌdʌznt 'mætər/

list *n* /lɪst/
lost *adj* /lɔst/

make *v* /meɪk/
make possible /ˌmeɪk 'pasəbl/
many more /ˌmɛni 'mor/
maybe *adv* /'meɪbi/
mean *v* /min/
military *adj* /'mɪləˌtɛri/

network *n* /'nɛtwərk/
north /nɔrθ/

often *adv* /'ɔfn/
other /'ʌðər/

partner *n* /'partnər/
passport *n* /'pæsport/
plan *v* /plæn/
plane (airplane) *n* /pleɪn ('ɛrpleɪn)/
problem *n* /'prabləm/
push *v* /pʊʃ/
put *v* /pʊt/

read *v* /rid/
really *adv* /'rili/
reservation *n* /ˌrɛzər'veɪʃn/
ride *v* /raɪd/
run *v* /rʌn/

slowly *adv* /'sloʊli/
song *n* /sɔŋ/
south /saʊθ/
start *v* /start/
stop *v* /stap/
swim *v* /swɪm/

tell me the time /ˌtɛl mi ðə 'taɪm/
thing *n* /θɪŋ/
ticket machine *n* /'tɪkət məˌʃin/
tractor *n* /'træktər/

understand *v* /ˌʌndər'stænd/
use *v* /yuz/

video *n* /'vɪdioʊ/

web *n* /wɛb/
web site *n* /'wɛbsaɪt/
well *adv* /wɛl/
word *n* /wərd/
worldwide *adv, adj* /wərld'waɪd/

you're welcome /yər 'wɛlkəm/

Unit 12

apple *n* /'æpl/
apple pie *n* /ˌæpl 'paɪ/
article *n* /'artɪkl/

birthday card *n* /'bərθdei ˌkard/
black coffee *n* /blæk kɔfi/
bottle *n* /batl/
burger *n* /'bərgər/

certainly *adv* /'sərtnli/
change *n* /tʃeɪndʒ/
cheese *n* /tʃiz/
chicken *n* /'tʃɪkən/
cup *n* /kʌp/

dessert *n* /dɪ'zərt/

feel at home /ˌfil ət 'hoʊm/
film (for a camera) *n* /fɪlm/
fish *n* /fɪʃ/
fries *n pl* /fraɪz/
fruit *n* /frut/

generation *n* /ˌdʒɛnə'reɪʃn/
get (= buy) *v* /gɛt/
granddaughter *n* /'grænˌdɔtər/

hairdresser *n* /'hɛrdrɛsər/

I'm just looking /ˌaɪm dʒəst 'lʊkɪŋ/
Indian *adj* /'ɪndiən/

junk food *n* /'dʒʌŋk fʊd/

kilo *n* /'kiloʊ/

large *adj* /lardʒ/
letter *n* /'lɛtər/

main course *n* /'meɪn ˌkɔrs/
meat *n* /mit/
medium *adj* /'midiəm/
menu *n* /'mɛnyu/
mineral water *n* /'mɪnərəl ˌwɔtr/
music store *n* /'myuzɪk ˌstɔr/

oldest *adj* /'oʊldəst/
only *adv* /'oʊnli/
order *v* /'ɔrdər/

pair of jeans *n* /ˌpɛr əv 'dʒinz/
person *n* /'pərsən/
phone card *n* /'foʊn kard/
popcorn *n* /'papkɔrn/
potato *n* /pə'teɪtoʊ/
program *n* /'proʊgræm/

roast (chicken) *adj* /roʊst/

shirt *n* /ʃərt/
side order *n* /'saɪd ˌɔrdər/
size *n* /saɪz/
small *adj* /smɔl/
sparkling water *n* /'sparklɪŋ ˌwɔtr/
stamp *n* /stæmp/
sugar *n* /ʃʊgər/

tomato *n* /tə'meɪtoʊ/
try *v* /traɪ/
try on *v* /ˌtraɪ 'an/

vegetable *n* /'vɛdʒtəbl/

(coffee) with milk /wɪθ 'mɪlk/

Unit 13

adult *n* /əˈdʌlt/
always *adv* /ˈɔlweɪz/
anything *adj* /ˈɛniθɪŋ/

barbecue *n* /ˈbɑrbɪkyu/
bathing suit *n* /ˈbeɪðɪŋ sut/
blonde *adj* /blɑnd/
boots *n pl* /bʊts/
bored *adj* /bɔrd/

church *n* /tʃərtʃ/
clothing *n* /ˈkloʊðɪŋ/
coat *n* /koʊt/

dress *n* /drɛs/
during *prep* /ˈdʊrɪŋ/

enjoy *v* /ɛnˈdʒɔɪ/
eye *n* /aɪ/

fashion show *n* /ˈfæʃən ˌʃoʊ/

get married /gɛt ˈmærid/
get ready /gɛt ˈrɛdi/
grandparent *n* /ˈgrænˌpɛrənt/

hair *n* /hɛr/
hat *n* /hæt/
hungry *adj* /ˈhʌngri/

interview *v* /ˈɪntərvyu/

jacket *n* /ˈdʒækɪt/

listener *n* /ˈlɪstənər/
love story *n* /ˈlʌv ˌstɔri/

meet *v* /mit/
model *n* /ˈmɑdəl/

New Year's Day *n* /nu yirz dei/

pack (bags) *v* /pæk (bæɡz)/
pants *n pl* /pænts/

read *v* /rid/
relax *v* /rɪˈlæks/

sandals *n pl* /ˈsændəlz/
shirt *n* /ʃərt/
shoes *n pl* /ʃuz/
short *adj* /ʃɔrt/
shorts *n pl* /ʃɔrts/
skirt *n* /skərt/
sneakers *n* /ˈsnikərz/
socks *n pl* /sɑks/
special *adj* /ˈspɛʃəl/
stand *v* /stænd/
study *v* /ˈstʌdi/
swim *n* /swɪm/

talk *v* /tɔk/
the news *n* /ðə ˈnuz/
thirsty *adj* /ˈθərsti/
tie *n* /taɪ/
tired *adj* /taɪərd/

wear *v* /wɛr/
what's the matter? /ˌwɑts ðə ˈmætr/
women *n pl* /ˈwɪmən/
write *v* /raɪt/

Colors

black /blæk/
blue /blu/
brown /braʊn/
gray /greɪ/
green /grin/
red /rɛd/
yellow /ˈyɛloʊ/
white /waɪt/

Unit 14

around *prep* /əˈraʊnd/
arrive *v* /əˈraɪv/

backpack *n* /ˈbækpæk/
bicycle *n* /ˈbaɪsɪkl/
bus tour *n* /ˈbʌs ˌtʊr/
busy *adj* /ˈbɪzi/

catch a plane /ˈkætʃ ə ˌpleɪn/
cost *v* /kɔst/
country and western *n* /ˈkʌntri ən ˌwɛstərn/
crazy about /ˈkreɪzi əˌbaʊt/

diary *n* /ˈdaɪəri/
DJ (disc jockey) *n* /ˈdidʒeɪ (ˈdɪsk dʒɑki)/

excited *adj* /ˌɛkˈsaɪtɪd/

flight *n* /flaɪt/
fly *v* /flaɪ/
future *n* /ˈfyutʃər/

go jogging /ˌgoʊ ˈdʒɑgɪŋ/
go sightseeing /ˌgoʊ ˈsaɪtsiɪŋ/

hostel *n* /ˈhɑstl/
hour *n* /aʊr/
how long? /ˌhaʊ ˈlɔŋ/
how nice! /ˌhaʊ ˈnaɪs/

it's time to go /ɪts ˌtaɪm tə ˈgoʊ/

jazz *n* /dʒæz/

land *n* /lænd/
last month /ˌlæst ˈmʌnθ/
lucky *adj* /ˈlʌki/

map *n* /mæp/
motorcycle *n* /ˈmoʊtərˌsaɪkl/
museum *n* /myuˈziəm/
musical *adj* /ˈmyuzɪkl/

New Zealand *n* /ˌnu ˈzilənd/

open *adj* /ˈoʊpən/
plan *n* /plæn/
pick up *v* /ˈpɪk əp/

ship *n* /ʃɪp/
soon *adv* /sun/
subway *n* /ˈsʌbweɪ/

the next one /ðə ˈnɛkst ˌwən/
ticket *n* /ˈtɪkɪt/
tour *n* /tʊr/
tourist *n* /ˈtʊrɪst/
travel agent *n* /ˈtrævl ˌeɪdʒənt/

visitor *n* /ˈvɪzətər/

Irregular Verbs

Base form	Past simple
be	was/were
bring	brought
buy	bought
can	could
come	came
cost	cost
do	did
draw	drew
drink	drank
drive	drove
eat	ate
feel	felt
find	found
fly	flew
forget	forgot
get	got
give	gave
go	went
have	had
know	knew
leave	left
make	made
mean	meant
meet	met
pay	paid
put	put
read /riːd/	read /rɛd/
ride	rode
run	ran
say	said
see	saw
sell	sold
send	sent
sit	sat
sleep	slept
speak	spoke
take	took
teach	taught
think	thought
understand	understood
wear	wore

Phonetic Symbols

Consonants			
1	/p/	as in	**pen** /pɛn/
2	/b/	as in	**big** /bɪg/
3	/t/	as in	**tea** /ti/
4	/d/	as in	**do** /du/
5	/k/	as in	**cat** /kæt/
6	/g/	as in	**go** /goʊ/
7	/f/	as in	**five** /faɪv/
8	/v/	as in	**very** /ˈvɛri/
9	/s/	as in	**son** /sʌn/
10	/z/	as in	**zoo** /zu/
11	/l/	as in	**live** /lɪv/
12	/m/	as in	**my** /maɪ/
13	/n/	as in	**nine** /naɪn/
14	/h/	as in	**happy** /ˈhæpi/
15	/r/	as in	**red** /rɛd/
16	/y/	as in	**yes** /yɛs/
17	/w/	as in	**want** /wɑnt/
18	/θ/	as in	**thanks** /θæŋks/
19	/ð/	as in	**the** /ðə/
20	/ʃ/	as in	**she** /ʃi/
21	/ʒ/	as in	**television** /ˈtɛləvɪʒn/
22	/tʃ/	as in	**child** /tʃaɪld/
23	/dʒ/	as in	**Japan** /dʒəˈpæn/
24	/ŋ/	as in	**English** /ˈɪŋglɪʃ/

Vowels			
25	/i/	as in	**see** /si/
26	/ɪ/	as in	**his** /hɪz/
27	/ɛ/	as in	**ten** /tɛn/
28	/æ/	as in	**stamp** /stæmp/
29	/ɑ/	as in	**father** /ˈfɑðər/
30	/ɔ/	as in	**morning** /ˈmɔrnɪŋ/
31	/ʊ/	as in	**book** /bʊk/
32	/u/	as in	**you** /yu/
33	/ʌ/	as in	**sun** /sʌn/
34	/ə/	as in	**about** /əˈbaʊt/
35	/eɪ/	as in	**name** /neɪm/
36	/aɪ/	as in	**my** /maɪ/
37	/ɔɪ/	as in	**boy** /bɔɪ/
38	/aʊ/	as in	**how** /haʊ/
39	/oʊ/	as in	**go** /goʊ/
40	/ər/	as in	**girl** /gərl/
41	/ɪr/	as in	**near** /nɪr/
42	/ɛr/	as in	**hair** /hɛr/
43	/ɑr/	as in	**car** /kɑr/
44	/ɔr/	as in	**more** /mɔr/
45	/ʊr/	as in	**tour** /tʊr/